HISTORY'S
VILLAINS

POL
POT

John Allen

BLACKBIRCH PRESS

An imprint of Thomson Gale, a part of The Thomson Corporation

THOMSON

GALE

Detroit • New York • San Francisco • San Diego • New Haven, Conn. • Waterville, Maine • London • Munich

© 2006 Thomson Gale, a part of The Thomson Corporation.

Thomson and Star Logo are trademarks and Gale and Blackbirch Press are registered trademarks used herein under license.

For more information, contact
Blackbirch Press
27500 Drake Rd.
Farmington Hills, MI 48331-3535
Or you can visit our Internet site at http://www.gale.com

LIBRARY OF CONGRESS CATALOGING-IN-PUBLICATION DATA

Allen, John, 1957–
  Pol Pot / by John Allen.
    p. cm. — (History's villains)
  Includes bibliographical references and index.
  ISBN 1-56711-901-8 (hardcover : alk. paper)
  1. Pol Pot—Juvenile literature. 2. Cambodia—Politics and government—20th century—Juvenile literature. 3. Prime ministers—Cambodia—Biography—Juvenile literature. I. Title. II. Series.

  DS554.83.P65A75 2005
  959.604'092—dc22   2005000393

Printed in the United States of America

CONTENTS

INTRODUCTION: HATRED AND PARANOIA   5

Chapter 1   THE ORIGINAL KHMER   7

Chapter 2   APPRENTICE TO COMMUNISM   24

Chapter 3   THE KHMER ROUGE   40

Chapter 4   POL POT COMES TO POWER   54

Chapter 5   THE KILLING FIELDS   71

Chapter 6   POL POT IN EXILE   86

CHRONOLOGY   103

GLOSSARY   106

SOURCE NOTES   108

FOR MORE INFORMATION   109

INDEX   110

PICTURE CREDITS   112

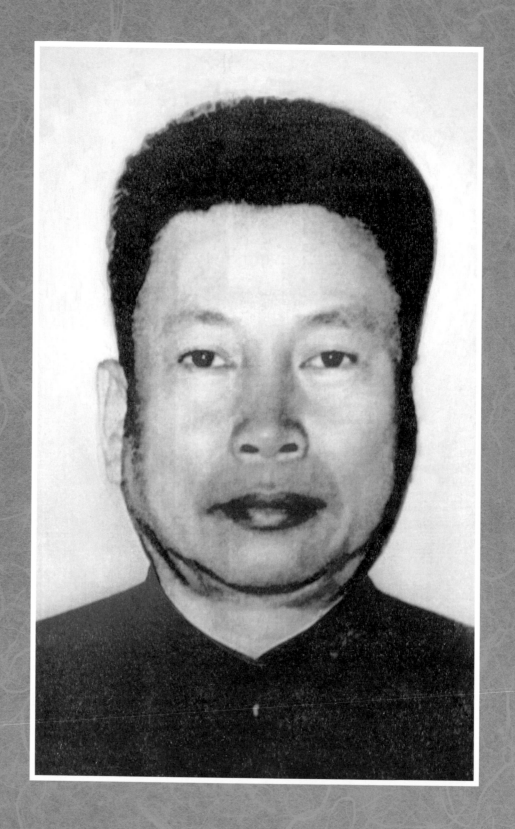

INTRODUCTION:
HATRED AND PARANOIA

In November 1978, three years after his rebel group seized power in Cambodia, the dictator Pol Pot could see the revolution crumbling around him. He was convinced that his enemies were everywhere. Vietnamese troops were making raids across the border in the east. Vietnamese planes were pounding Pol Pot's rebel troops, the Khmer Rouge. Thousands of Cambodians were fleeing into Vietnam or joining the homegrown forces gathering to oppose Pol Pot. In this atmosphere, no one could be trusted, not even his former friends and colleagues.

A shackled prisoner was brought before Pol Pot. His name was Vorn Vet, and he had served as deputy prime minister for the economy in Democratic Kampuchea, as Cambodia was called during the revolution. Vorn Vet had been a colleague of Pol Pot since the 1950s, when they had begun the long struggle to overthrow the corrupt government of Norodom Sihanouk. Their past

Between 1975 and 1979, Pol Pot led a dictatorship in Cambodia that claimed the lives of more than 1 million people.

friendship, however, counted for nothing. Charges accusing Vorn Vet of plotting against the regime had been wrung from a torture victim in an interrogation at Tuol Sleng, the notorious prison in Phnom Penh. The charges were flimsy, pure hearsay at best, yet Vorn Vet was given no opportunity to rebut them. The accusation alone was sufficient to convict him in the eyes of his former friend.

Confronted with this accused traitor, the usually composed Pol Pot could not restrain his fury. He set upon the shackled prisoner and beat him so ferociously that he broke the prisoner's leg. Then Vorn Vet was himself sent to Tuol Sleng, where he was tortured and executed within days. He was but one of thousands of victims who had supported the revolution only to be murdered for some trumped-up offense. The hatred and paranoia of the Khmer Rouge and its leader knew no bounds. To Pol Pot, one death meant nothing. Only the revolution mattered.

CHAPTER 1

THE ORIGINAL KHMER

Cambodia is one of three Southeast Asian countries that fell under French rule in the late nineteenth century. The others are Vietnam, which borders Cambodia on the east, and Laos, on Cambodia's northern border. This linked group of countries became known as Indochina.

In the second half of the twentieth century, the people of Indochina lived in almost constant turmoil. One group after another fought for control or influence in these countries. Outside powers such as France, China, and the United States vied with internal factions, including royalists, Democrats, and Communists. War and rebellion became a way of life.

In 1975 a Communist group called the Khmer Rouge, or the Red Khmer, seized power in Cambodia. The group's leaders declared a new beginning to Cambodian history—"Year Zero," they called it. Rebel troops emptied the cities at gunpoint. Aristocrats and intellectuals were shot immediately. Hundreds of thousands of others were forced to march into the

Waving his pistol, a Khmer Rouge soldier threatens a crowd of people in Phnom Penh during the Communist takeover of Cambodia in 1975.

countryside and work on farms. Hospitals, factories, and schools were all shut down. Libraries were ransacked. For four years, the Cambodian people lost the freedom to speak, write, meet, own property, or worship. Those who disobeyed the Khmer Rouge's rules were shot, as were thousands of non-Cambodians. Many perished from hunger or overwork. In all, an estimated 1.5 million people, about one-fourth of the total population, died under the Khmer Rouge.

The architect of this catastrophe was a lifelong rebel named Pol Pot. To this day, Pol Pot remains a mysterious figure. Although mild-mannered and soft-spoken, he had an iron will and an uncanny ability to sway his followers. His story begins in rural Cambodia, among rice paddies and simple farmhouses.

Khmer Roots

The real name of the man who became Pol Pot was Saloth Sar. He was born on May 25, 1928, the eighth of nine children. His village near Kompong Thom lay ninety miles north of the capital city, Phnom Penh. His parents were Khmer, or rural Cambodians. More than 90 percent of the Cambodian people are Khmer.

Like most Khmer, Sar's parents farmed in the countryside. Their red-tiled house sat on stilts overlooking a brown river lined with mango and coconut trees. Sar's father, Pen Saloth, was prosperous as a farmer. He owned sizable fields of rice and garden land and six buffalo. Sar's mother, Sok Nem, was known for miles around as a pious woman ready to help others.

As an adult, Sar often claimed that he had worked in the fields, but that was not true. At age six, he and his older brother Saloth Chhay were sent to live with relatives in Phnom Penh. There, Sar lived among symbols of Cambodia's impressive past.

From Angkor to French Rule

Much of Cambodia's modern history is an attempt to recapture past glories. Beginning about A.D. 800, a remarkable Khmer kingdom arose in Cambodia. Its leaders excelled in warfare and construction. They dredged reservoirs and channels to collect the floodwaters of the Mekong River for better farming. They also built beautiful temples to promote the Hindu and Buddhist faiths. Each religion had its followers among the Khmer. The kingdom became known as Angkor, or "holy city," for its impressive capital.

In the early 1100s, a Khmer king built Angkor Wat, a huge temple that covers five hundred acres. With its intricate carvings and reflecting moat, the sandstone

THE GEOGRAPHY OF CAMBODIA

Cambodia is a small country of about 69,000 square miles (180,000 sq. km). It is slightly smaller than the U.S. state of Oklahoma. It lies about 12 degrees north of the equator—roughly the latitude of Nicaragua. Cambodia is bordered by three countries—Thailand to the northwest, Laos to the northeast, and Vietnam to the east and southeast. The Gulf of Thailand washes along its southwestern border.

Cambodia's climate is warm and wet. Twice a year, the country is hit by monsoons, or tropical storms with torrential rains. In the rainy seasons, villages become islands in temporary lakes of rainwater. Temperatures in the hottest months average 95°F, and even when the cooler monsoon breezes prevail they rarely drop below 68°F. The heat and standing water form a perfect breeding ground for malaria-carrying mosquitoes.

The rolling landscape of Cambodia is mostly made up of flatlands and sloping hills called *phnoms* in the Khmer language. In the border regions, mountains and thick jungles abound. The Mekong River slices through the eastern half of Cambodia, while its tributary, the Sap River, flows from the Tonle Sap, or Great Lake, in northwestern Cambodia.

With fertile soil and plentiful water, Cambodia is ideal for farming. Flat stretches of land retain water for the marsh-like paddies where rice is cultivated. Sloping hills are terraced to allow rice farming in other areas. Cambodian farmers can produce three or four rice crops a year, enough for a healthy surplus that can be sold for export.

structure marked the high point of Angkor civilization. Soon after its completion, however, Angkor kings began to lose power to Thai and Vietnamese rivals. In 1431, Thai armies sacked Angkor and ended the Khmer empire. The once-grand temples were engulfed by jungle overgrowth.

For the next four centuries, Cambodia's weakened kings relied more and more on alliances with Thailand or Vietnam to maintain power. By the mid-1800s, Cambodia faced annexation by Vietnam. It was saved only by the arrival of a new power in the region: France.

In 1859, French armies captured Saigon, the main city in Vietnam. Using it as a base, France went on to secure the rest of Vietnam as its colony. In 1863 the French forced Cambodia's King Norodom to sign over control of his kingdom. France installed a consul, or officer, to oversee its interests in Cambodia. Thirty years later, France also added Laos to its colonial holdings.

French Influence in Cambodia

France claimed to be bringing civilization to its Asian colonies. Christian missionaries fanned out to convert the people. In reality, however, the French mainly sought profit from Vietnam and stability in the rest of Indochina. They introduced industry to the region, and as a result people began moving from farms to the cities. In Cambodia, French export houses prospered from trade in Cambodian rubber, fish, timber, rice, and corn. Many Chinese and Vietnamese traders also grew rich. Cambodians, however, were slow to adjust to trade and business. For the most part, the new prosperity bypassed them.

The elite Khmer went to modern French schools and learned about French history and culture. In turn, the French helped the Khmer appreciate their own history. French explorers and scientists discovered Angkor Wat and other splendid old temples. They translated inscriptions from remote ruins. Soon they had pieced together the history of the great Khmer empire—a history that Cambodians themselves had forgotten. As a result, Cambodians came to realize that they had not always bowed down to foreign powers.

In the 1930s feelings of national pride were also stirred by the appearance of the first newspaper in the Khmer language. Its editorials urged Cambodians to compete harder with Chinese shopkeepers and Vietnamese workers. The French consul did not object to such ideas, mainly because the country remained firmly under French control. When Cambodia's King Monivong died in 1941, the consul chose the king's

13

nineteen-year-old grandson as a replacement. Norodom Sihanouk seemed an ideal choice—a figurehead who would defer to French rule.

A Buddhist Monastery and a Catholic School

In 1934, seven years before Sihanouk ascended to the throne, Saloth Sar arrived in Phnom Penh. At that time, French rule was taken for granted. Sar often heard grumblings about the French, yet no one dared oppose them openly.

Sar first entered a Buddhist monastery near the royal palace. His head was shaved and he wore yellow robes. Monks taught the boy the basic ideas

King Norodom Sihanouk (left), seen here with French officials in 1948, was a puppet ruler controlled by the French.

of Buddhism. He also learned to read his native Khmer language. Discipline at the monastery was very strict, and every order had to be obeyed.

After a year, Sar moved on to a Catholic school. He learned to speak French and became well-versed in Catholicism, the religion of the French rulers. His classmates were mostly the children of French bureaucrats or Vietnamese traders. They remembered Sar as polite and quiet, with an even temper. There were no fights with other students, no outbursts or tantrums. "The contemptible Pot," said his brother Loth Suong, "was a lovely child."[1]

High School in Kompong Cham

In 1942 Saloth Sar entered a newly created boarding school in Kompong Cham, Cambodia's third largest city. The school was named for Norodom Sihanouk, the new king. The first class was limited to an elite group of twenty boys from various provinces. Classes included history, geography, mathematics, literature, and philosophy. Sar and the other boys spoke French exclusively. They even played musical instruments and performed comedies.

Although pleasant and well-liked by the other boys, Sar was nothing special as a student. He enjoyed games, but was not particularly good at them. One of Sar's classmates later recalled that he thought a lot but said very little.

A Taste of Independence

At this time, many Cambodian students were thinking about political events. In 1942, French authorities arrested two Buddhist monks for preaching sermons about nationalism—the idea that the people of a nation should rule themselves and resist outside influence. The monks urged Cambodians to take back control of the country. Their arrest set off a flood of protests. Hundreds of monks and thousands of civilians filled the streets of the normally quiet capital. A riot broke out, and several monks were arrested and imprisoned. It was the first grassroots protest in the history of Cambodia.

The end of World War II caused further upheaval. Since 1940 France had been occupied by Nazi Germany. The Vichy government installed by the Nazis took charge of French colonies, including Cambodia. The armies of Japan, Germany's ally in the war, conquered most of Southeast Asia, but the Japanese allowed the Vichy officials to remain in Cambodia. When France was liberated by the Allied powers in 1944, Japan took action in Cambodia. The Japanese jailed French officials and ordered Sihanouk to declare independence from France.

The taste of independence was brief. When Japan surrendered, the French returned to Cambodia.

Although a majority of Cambodians now opposed French rule, Sihanouk himself welcomed them back. He relied on French arms to keep him in power, and he had come to love French culture and comforts. To appease the nationalists, French officials allowed them to create a new Cambodian constitution, political parties, and a national assembly. With these changes, the French hoped to prevent the violent rebellions against their rule that were erupting in Vietnam from spreading to Cambodia.

Technical School and a Voyage to France

Sar followed these events closely. Nevertheless, politics had yet to become the focus of his life. In 1948, he enrolled in carpentry classes at a technical school in Phnom Penh. His move marked a break with most of his former classmates. While they qualified for a prestigious school called the Lycée Sisowath, Sar failed the exams necessary for entrance.

During this time, Sar met Ieng Sary, who went to Lycée Sisowath. Sary, the son of a well-to-do landowner, was an excellent student. While on scholarship at the Lycée Sisowath, Sary became fascinated with politics. He joined the new Democratic Party in Cambodia, along with many monks, teachers, and civil servants. The Democrats wanted Cambodia to be an independent nation in which the people selected their own leaders. Under Sary's influence, Sar also joined the Democrats and worked for the party in its successful campaign for the new national assembly.

In 1949, Ieng Sary (pictured) encouraged the young Saloth Sar to join Cambodia's newly formed Democratic Party.

In 1949, Sar unexpectedly received a scholarship to study in France, granted by the new prime minister, a Democrat who wanted to show his gratitude for Sar's work on his campaign. In August, Sar and twenty other scholars sailed from Saigon for the monthlong voyage. When he left to study in Paris, Sar joined an elite group of Cambodians. Most came from influential families, and were expected to play important roles in Cambodian affairs.

The Lure of Communism

Sar relished his new life in the bustling city of Paris. Soon he was enrolled in a technical school, taking classes on radio electricity. He rented a room in the Indochinese section of a dormitory for foreign students.

During his stay in Paris, Sar met two Cambodians named Thiounn Mumm and Keng Vannsak. Both were talented young men who relished the lively conversations that took place in smoky Paris cafés. Art, literature, politics, and philosophy were all subjects for passionate debate among students. One of the hottest topics was the political system called communism.

Communism was based on the ideas of a nineteenth-century German named Karl Marx. Marx thought that property and goods should not be owned and exchanged by individuals, but rather by the government. He insisted that capitalism, an economic system based on private ownership, was unfair to ordinary workers. The weight of this unfairness, Marx thought, would cause workers to overthrow the capitalist system and replace it with communism. Under communism, everyone would work together toward the same goals. Government would eventually become unnecessary and wither away.

Marx and his friend Friedrich Engels expressed these ideas in a book called *The Communist Manifesto* (1848). In 1917, Communists led by Vladimir Lenin took over the government of Russia and established the Soviet

19

Union. Many intellectuals saw the Soviet Union, led by Lenin's successor, Joseph Stalin, as the best hope for a better world. They were not aware of (or chose to ignore) the facts about Stalin's rule. Far from a worker's paradise, the Soviet Union was a morass of poverty, famine, and political terror. Millions died as a result of Stalin's policies. His system of concentration camps, called the gulag, held hundreds of thousands of innocent Russians.

Nevertheless, in the years after World War II, many young people thought communism was the solution to the world's problems. Saloth Sar joined the debate upon his arrival in Paris. It was not long before he acted upon his new interest in politics.

Trip to Yugoslavia

In the summer of 1950, Sar got his first glimpse of communism in action. He and several other Cambodians in Paris volunteered for a monthlong trip to Yugoslavia. Under its leader, Marshal Tito, Yugoslavia had broken free from the Soviet Union's influence. Tito was trying to start his own brand of communism. Results were mixed at best. Attempts to collectivize peasant farms had mostly failed. Food shortages ravaged the country. Yet Tito mobilized huge numbers of

Yugoslav citizens to work on public building projects such as roads and hospitals. Sar himself worked alongside the people.

The idea of solving national problems by urging citizens to work harder appealed to Sar. He admired the Yugoslav people for their energy and perseverance in the lean years after World War II. Communism, Sar decided, could be a powerful force for unity.

A Discussion Group in Paris

Ideas of Communist revolution swirled in Sar's head. When his friend Ieng Sary came to Paris, Sar moved to a new room near him and Keng Vannsak. Ignoring his schoolwork, Sar read books published by the French Communist Party. Soon he was joining his friends in political meetings.

At these evening meetings, their circle would discuss Marx's writings and other books on communism. Heated speakers would switch back and forth between French and the Khmer language. Members of the group also kept an eye on events back home in Cambodia. Arguments raged about the best way to bring the revolution to their homeland. A feeling of secrecy and excitement pervaded the stuffy apartments where these discussions were held.

Those who attended the meetings disagree about Saloth Sar's role. Some recall him as mostly listening and keeping in the background. Others insist that Sar played a primary part from the beginning. The differences among stories show Sar's contradictory personality: He seemed to wear a different mask for every situation.

Around this time, Sar also met his future wife, Khieu Ponnary. She was the daughter of a judge and eight years older than Sar. Her degree from the Lycée Sisowath was an unusual achievement for a Cambodian woman of that time. In Paris, she became a respected teacher. She also shared the radical politics of her Cambodian friends.

A Fiery Article

Political events in Cambodia inspired Saloth Sar's first published article, a fiery piece titled "Monarchy or Democracy?" Sar signed it *Khmer daom,* or "Original Khmer." He hoped to align himself with the Khmer— the peasants and rural workers in Cambodia. His friend Keng Vannsak had the piece published at once in a left-wing magazine.

In the article, Sar railed against Sihanouk. With French help, Sihanouk had abolished the national assembly and declared himself sole ruler. To Sar, he was a traitor to the people. The monarchy's only purpose, he said, was to "exploit the majority of the people at every level."[2] Sar compared peasants in Cambodia to animals made to work day and night to feed the royal circle. What Cambodia needed, Sar wrote, was a true government of the people. He urged the people to revolt, and cited revolutions in France, Russia, and China as models of democracy.

Sihanouk was quick to respond to Sar's article. He cut off scholarships for all students associated with the magazine and with other protests against his coup. Even Keng Vannsak, who had relatives in Sihanouk's government, was ordered home.

Saloth Sar had already lost his scholarship months before. Academically, he had fared no better than he did in Cambodian schools. Classes meant nothing to him, and he never took an examination. By the time he returned home to Cambodia in 1952, he had joined the French Communist Party.

CHAPTER 2

APPRENTICE TO COMMUNISM

$\mathscr{B}$ack home in Phnom Penh, Saloth Sar prepared for a career as a Communist subversive. His goal was to overthrow the government in Cambodia. Much of his work would be done in the shadows, away from the prying eyes of government police. He would take orders from party leaders and try to recruit new members. Every day would demand patience and discipline. For the first time, Sar's life had a purpose.

Soon after his return, Sar contacted the local representative of the Indochina Communist Party (ICP), which was made up mainly of Vietnamese members. Sar's background in the French Communist

Dressed in peasant's clothing, Saloth Sar poses for a photo in a field to project the image that he is a man of the people.

Party was checked and approved. He began work for the ICP immediately.

The Vietminh

The ICP cell, or outpost, that Sar joined was in eastern Cambodia, on the border with Vietnam. Half of this cell consisted of Khmer, and the other half consisted of North Vietnamese guerrilla fighters called Vietminh. The Vietminh had been struggling to oust the French from Indochina for almost a decade. They claimed leadership over the entire Communist movement in Indochina.

Sar's first jobs were menial, including kitchen work and hauling fertilizer. Steadily, however, he was given more to do. Despite the fact that Sar did not speak Vietnamese and had no fighting experience, the Vietminh saw potential in the new recruit. His ties with radicals in France made up for his failings in school. Most of all, the Vietminh were impressed with his enthusiasm. Alone among his Communist friends, Sar had hiked to the frontier to work for the ICP.

In November 1953, Sihanouk convinced the French to grant independence to Cambodia. In a special ceremony, French troops marched out of the capital. Sihanouk was proving to be a formidable figure in politics, able to garner support from many different factions. Most Democrats in Cambodia gave their support to him, while the Communists watched and waited.

A Communist Mentor

Patience came easy to Saloth Sar. Gradually, as he learned more about the party's organization, he moved up in the ICP and was given more responsibilities. A key figure in his education was an older man named Tou Samouth.

Samouth was a Khmer from Cochinchina, a southern region of Vietnam. He had become a monk during World War II, but later abandoned his calling to join the Vietminh. As a propagandist and teacher, Samouth was known for his speeches to Khmer recruits. He patiently led them, step by step, through the coming class struggle. Workers would be the base, joined by teachers, students, and peasants. He warned recruits about the enemies of the revolution, including Sihanouk, the French, and the Americans, who staunchly opposed Communist movements throughout the world.

As a role model, Tou Samouth appealed to Sar. His quiet demeanor, idealism, and passion for teaching impressed the younger man. Sar also approved of Samouth's Buddhist background, which, with its links to Cambodian history and everyday peasant life, seemed fitting for a Khmer revolutionary. In a later interview, Sar said of Samouth, "He made me so happy, and I believed in him. When he opened a study course, I tried hard to understand him, and when he went out on propaganda missions, I followed along after him. This awakened me to the clear realities of the revolution."[3] The two began to work closely together.

The Geneva Settlement

In 1955, the political struggle of Samouth and other Cambodian Communists was rocked by an important agreement that was reached in Geneva, Switzerland, that

27

A Vietnamese soldier safe on the ground watches as fellow paratroopers drop into position during the Battle of Dien Bien Phu in 1953.

affected all sides in the political struggle. Members of the United Nations Security Council launched talks to end the First Indochina War. This conflict between the French and Ho Chi Minh's resistance army in Vietnam had started in 1946. After years of fighting, the tide had turned against the French. They were anxious to approve a face-saving settlement.

The settlement divided Vietnam at the 17th parallel. National elections were ordered, with the understanding that the north would probably become a Communist state. The south became the Republic of Vietnam. Vietminh fighters in the south were given the choice either to resettle in the north or drop their arms and try to gain support by political means.

The Geneva agreement, which recognized France's diminished role in the region, also called for a new round of elections in Cambodia. Unlike those in the late 1940s, these elections would be free of French influence. Parties geared up for a historic campaign. With strong support nationwide, the Democrats saw a chance to gain real power. Meanwhile, Sihanouk felt slighted. His crusade for independence already seemed forgotten. Nevertheless, he remained the most powerful political figure in Cambodia. Also, he commanded a formidable police force, which could deal with the most troublesome opposition parties.

Behind the Scenes

Meanwhile, Saloth Sar was learning how to exert his own influence. He worked constantly on party business. Behind the scenes, Sar helped Keng Vannsak and others to radicalize the Democratic Party, or replace its leaders with those closer to the Communists' viewpoint. He then served as contact between the Democrats and the ICP. At this time, he operated under a false name—

indeed, under several different names. Most frequently, he used the name Pol, the Cambodian form of Paul. His transformation into the mysterious revolutionary mastermind named Pol Pot was nearly complete.

In truth, Pol Pot had no desire for a Democratic victory. His goal was for Communists to take over in Cambodia. He knew that reaching that goal might require help from the Vietminh, Vietnam's Communist revolutionaries. Despite his misgivings about the Vietnamese, Pol Pot was willing to enlist them as allies in the revolution.

Vietnam and Cambodia had long had a strained relationship. Vietnam was like an older brother who patronized his younger sibling. The Vietnamese considered themselves more sophisticated and more advanced than the rustic Khmer. In the same way, Vietnamese revolutionaries treated their Cambodian counterparts as novices who must be led by the hand. Also, the two groups differed in which revolutionary model to emulate: The Vietnamese looked to the Soviet Union, while Pol Pot chose China. Pol Pot and the Cambodians distrusted the Vietnamese and even feared they might someday attempt a takeover. Still, Pol Pot could not deny the Vietminh's greater experience in spreading the Communist movement.

Such calculations showed a new seriousness in Pol Pot. He struck his friends as more intelligent and self-possessed than the quiet young man in those smoky Paris apartments. Certainly he was more committed— and unshakably convinced that his answers to society's problems were the only correct ones.

Sihanouk the Candidate

Fears about communism drove Sihanouk to crack down on his opponents. They also led him to join the campaign as a private citizen seeking office, a move that startled the nation. The party he formed, the Sangkum, borrowed the other candidates' most popular ideas. Sihanouk used intimidation, forcing Democrats on his government's payroll to support him or lose their jobs. Newspapers deemed too radical were shut down and their editors jailed.

Sihanouk railed against his opponents, most of whom he painted as Communists. Nevertheless, Cambodian voters swarmed to rallies for the Democrats. They cheered as Keng Vannsak criticized the idea of a birthright king and pointed out corruption in the royal circle.

At last, Sihanouk grew desperate. He realized that few of his party's candidates shared his charisma. The election results he needed were still not assured. The

King Sihanouk, seen here delivering a radio broadcast, used violence and intimidation to control his political enemies.

day before the election, Vannsak and other Democrats were arrested and held without bail. Democratic rallies were broken up by force.

The violence and intimidation worked. Citizens either cast their ballots for Sihanouk or stayed away from the polls altogether. The king's victory set the course for Cambodia's government for a generation. The new National Assembly of Cambodia served as a rubber stamp for his decrees. Pol Pot, Sihanouk's opposite in style and belief, returned to his secret work. His vision of a Communist victory would have to wait.

A New Profession

While work for the party was Pol Pot's true calling, he needed a daily job to support himself. He hit upon the ideal job for his situation: teaching. It allowed him to indoctrinate students with radical ideas while still maintaining his cover as an ordinary citizen. Despite his undistinguished school career, Pol Pot was able to make use of his many connections to get a teaching job.

Pol Pot joined a newly established high school in Phnom Penh called Chamraon Vichea, which means "progressive knowledge." There he taught history, geography, civics, and French. He quickly gained a reputation as an excellent teacher. Many of his students revered him as they would a wise Buddhist monk. Years later, they would describe the professor in his short-sleeved white shirt and dark blue trousers. They recalled his smooth, kindly features, his deep voice, and his ability to speak eloquently without sounding pretentious. They also responded to his calls for honesty and justice in their country. Teachers held a high place in Cambodian culture, and Pol Pot tapped into this natural respect. Chamraon Vichea quietly became a haven for radical teachers and a production line for radical youth.

Marriage to Khieu Ponnary

At home, Pol Pot could share his Communist plans with Khieu Ponnary. She taught literature at the Lycée Sisowath. The couple had grown closer when they worked on the Democrats' campaign. Not long afterward,

Pol Pot and Ponnary were married in a private ceremony. A small, neat woman, Ponnary refused all frills. She wore her hair in an old-fashioned style, dressed simply, and never appeared in jewelry or makeup. The couple's house was spotless, with almost no furniture or books. Unlike most families of their social class, they had no servants; their ideology would not allow it. They rarely socialized, and when they did, it was with Pol Pot's friend Ieng Sary and his wife.

By Cambodian standards, the marriage was rather odd. Men seldom chose brides who were older than themselves—certainly not eight years older. By the same token, women of Ponnary's social class rarely married men with so few prospects and so little money. Ponnary was drawn to the same qualities that attracted Pol Pot's students—his ideas, his commitment, and his hopes for the future.

The Life of a Revolutionary

Working for a Communist future required a great deal of stealth and cleverness in the present. Pol Pot met secretly with party members from inside and outside Cambodia. Few people knew about his double life.

Pol Pot had long since settled into the life of a revolutionary. He prided himself on his patience and iron discipline. Almost every day he was conducting secret meetings, passing on information, or smuggling pamphlets and messages. A rash word to the wrong person could result in imprisonment, yet Pol Pot operated without interference from Sihanouk's police. His bland features and calm demeanor deflected prying eyes. His position as a respected teacher served as the perfect cover. While his progressive opinions were known, they caused him no difficulty. Pol Pot proved to be a rarity among revolutionaries—he never saw the inside of a jail cell.

Pol Pot, in hiding as a Communist revolutionary, grants an interview to an American news team in the Cambodian jungle.

To protect himself further, Pol Pot also cut ties with his family. His last display of family feeling was when he attended his father's funeral in 1959. He also abandoned close friends such as Keng Vannsak. Nothing would interfere with his secret work.

Pol Pot's new friends came from the ranks of the Communist Party. Nuon Chea was a Chinese Khmer who had joined the party in Thailand. As Pol Pot worked in urban areas, Chea's responsibility was in the countryside. Like Pol Pot's other friends and mentors, Chea was intelligent and determined, with a lifelong fondness for radical ideas. Together with his tireless friend, he worked to connect a network of Communists in Cambodia.

A Party Congress

An important milestone for this network was a meeting held in the Phnom Penh railroad station in 1960. Members referred to it as a "party congress." Twenty-one delegates attended, fourteen from rural areas, seven from the cities. It was a dangerous gathering, for had it been discovered by Sihanouk's police, the party's leadership would have been destroyed.

The congress approved rules for the party and planned a long-term strategy for Communist takeover.

It also named the party the Workers' Party of Kampuchea (the native form of the word *Cambodia*). The party itself, it was decided, must continue in secret. Finally, members named a central committee that included Tou Samouth as secretary, Nuon Chea as deputy secretary, and Pol Pot as Samouth's assistant.

Death of the Party Secretary

Instructions from Vietnam often played havoc with the new party. For example, the Vietnamese recommended that the Cambodian Communists openly confront Sihanouk's government. Pol Pot and the committee thought this was suicide. Without arms and training, they had no chance of success. Yet the committee's disagreement with the Vietnamese sowed mistrust among members who revered the Vietminh radicals and considered them much wiser than their fellow Cambodians.

In July 1962, Tou Samouth, the new party secretary, was kidnapped from his safe house in Phnom Penh and murdered. It was widely assumed that Sihanouk's agents killed Samouth. The true story, however, remains uncertain. Some observers insist that Pol Pot was responsible, and certainly he was quick to benefit from his mentor's death. The committee chose him to be the acting secretary general.

Seminars and Crackdowns

In his new position, Pol Pot spoke with an authority he had never had before. While the party's activities remained generally secret, few among Cambodia's political left had not heard of Pol Pot—if not by name, then certainly by reputation as the prime organizer of radicals in the country. Pol Pot capitalized on this authority in the seminars he held to recruit new members of the faithful.

The seminars were not large gatherings. About fifty monks, teachers, bureaucrats, and other intellectuals attended each one. These people considered themselves Cambodia's elite. While they could picture themselves leading Khmer peasants to a glorious Communist future, they disdained the idea of working alongside such simple people. Even Pol Pot's relationship with the proletariat, or working people, was mainly theoretical. He simply assumed that they would welcome the changes the revolution would bring.

In the seminars, Pol Pot pointed out the inequities of Sihanouk's economic policies. Sihanouk had nationalized, or put under government control, many industries, including banking and foreign trade. He claimed to be helping the Khmer take a larger role in business. In reality, however, Sihanouk merely granted monopolies and special favors to his richest, most loyal supporters.

Ordinary Khmer saw no benefits, and many actually lost ground to Chinese and Vietnamese competitors.

Ideas of protest against Sihanouk's government spilled over from the seminars to after-school discussion groups. Some teachers passed along the Communists' message to their students. In 1963, protests broke out in three cities. Students paraded with signs that announced, "The Sangkum is rotten!"[4] In one demonstration, a student was killed and several others were injured.

Cambodians waited to see how Sihanouk, who was out of the country when the uprisings occurred, would react. He ordered his security chief, Lon Nol, to investigate. Nol compiled a list of subversives suspected of being Communists. The name Saloth Sar was included, along with those of four other high officials in the party. Pol Pot's double life came to an end.

To save himself, Pol Pot fled Phnom Penh and hid in the countryside in a region northeast of the capital. The government had forced his hand. Now he would devote every waking minute to the revolution in Cambodia. To his followers, he became "Brother Number One," the mastermind of the coming revolt.

CHAPTER 3

THE KHMER ROUGE

The next seven years (1963–1970) comprised the most difficult period of Pol Pot's life. His main concern was to stay one step ahead of Sihanouk's forces. He and his fellow revolutionaries hid in temporary camps in eastern and northeastern Cambodia. Most of the time they were cut off from the outside world. What little news filtered through came from party messengers and shortwave radio broadcasts.

Isolation bred a distorted view of reality. Pol Pot and his followers saw themselves as powerful agents of change in Cambodia, while most of their fellow citizens scarcely noticed their activities. Pol Pot spoke only with other members of the committee or visiting Communists. He never heard the practical opinions of genuine Khmer. Day after day he worked on elaborate plans to topple his enemies and bring "the people" to power. Subordinates around him fed his ego by praising every statement or idea. No one, not even committee members, would dare to contradict him. For Pol Pot the teacher, everyone else was required to be an attentive student.

In the remote forests of the northeast, Pol Pot and his band battled malaria, boredom, lack of resources, and discouragement. Success often must have seemed like a pipe dream to the Khmer Rouge—as Sihanouk called their movement. (Red, or the French *rouge*, is the traditional color to denote communism.) Yet somehow they hung together and waited for their chance to topple the government.

As they waited, the leaders of the Khmer Rouge became virtual prisoners of the Vietminh. These Vietnamese Communists guarded their mobile camp, which was known as Office 100.

Throughout the 1960s, Pol Pot was forced to hide in remote parts of Cambodia to avoid King Sihanouk's forces.

No Khmer Rouge, not even Pol Pot, could leave the camp without permission. They lacked arms and military supplies. The Cambodians, for all their brave talk, felt humiliated at their powerlessness.

The War in Vietnam

Meanwhile, a different power struggle raged on in Vietnam. The Communists in North Vietnam were fighting to unite the two halves of the country under a Communist government. Guerrillas in the south, part of the National Liberation Front, battled South Vietnam's government forces with sabotage and surprise attacks. To prevent a Communist takeover, the United States was providing assistance to South Vietnam—both in training and personnel. Soon the United States had replaced France as the key Western power in the region.

Sihanouk feared that if Cambodia were drawn into the war, it might be lost as a sovereign nation. He forged an alliance with North Vietnam and its allies in the south. By then, Sihanouk's hatred for the United States outweighed his distrust of Communists. He secretly allowed the Vietnamese Communists to set up camps inside Cambodia and have safe passage across the country's borders. To the Khmer Rouge, Sihanouk said, "I warn the Khmer Rouge that I will leave them to go about their filthy business freely so long as it does not threaten the vital interests of the nation."[5]

Sihanouk's decision encouraged the Vietnamese to demand military support from the Khmer Rouge. Without Sihanouk's knowledge, hundreds of Khmer radicals traveled to North Vietnam for training and indoctrination. Among them was Pol Pot.

Trip to Hanoi

With the war in South Vietnam escalating, the North Vietnamese hoped to enlist Pol Pot as an ally in their struggle. In late 1964, Pol Pot, along with several fellow Cambodians, crossed into Laos and traveled up the Ho Chi Minh Trail, a supply route named for the north's leader. Arriving in Hanoi, the North Vietnamese capital, Pol Pot met with his hosts and with Cambodian Communists who had relocated to Vietnam in 1954. These included friends he had scarcely seen since his stay in Paris.

In Hanoi, Pol Pot was treated with restrained politeness. The Vietnamese obviously wanted to coordinate their war effort with the Cambodian struggle. Nevertheless, Pol Pot was not pleased with his hosts' superior airs. Years later, he wrote the *Livre Noir* (*Black Book*), a bitter record of his meetings in the north. In it he described how Le Duan, the general secretary of the

Vietnamese Communist Party, had lectured him on the proper role for Cambodians in the revolution. Duan called on Pol Pot to renounce armed conflict in Cambodia and wait for the Vietnamese to win their war. Pol Pot felt that Duan feared losing control of the Cambodian movement. Despite his resentment, Pol Pot swallowed his pride and calmly agreed with the Vietnamese leader. He realized that had he not agreed, Duan probably would have found a way to remove him as leader of the Khmer Rouge.

A Visit to Mao's China

Pol Pot then expressed a desire to continue on to Beijing. He long had wished to see the result of Mao Tse-tung's 1949 Communist revolution in China. The Chinese, as strong supporters of Vietnam's war effort against the United States, finally decided to interview this rising revolutionary from Cambodia; perhaps he could be of some help to their cause. After months of waiting, Pol Pot finally was granted permission to travel to Beijing.

The trip influenced Pol Pot in many ways. His Chinese hosts boosted his ego by treating him with great respect. The crowded cities, huge celebrations, and massive building projects he witnessed in Beijing confirmed his revolutionary feelings. Here was an example of what the people, led by the Communist Party, could do. He admired Mao's ideas, such as his focus on bringing the poorest peasants into the revolution and his encouragement of continuous class warfare. Pol Pot also liked the simplicity of Mao's *Little Red Book*, a volume of quotes from his speeches chosen to appeal to people who could barely read.

Of course, Pol Pot saw only what his hosts wanted him to see. Certainly he was predisposed to look favorably on a peasant-based revolution. What he did not

Chinese Communist leader Mao Tse-tung (left) meets with Khmer Rouge leaders Pol Pot (background) and Ieng Sary (right) in 1970.

see—or refused to acknowledge—was the awful human toll of the revolution in China. In the first years alone, more than 3 million people had been murdered for dissenting against the Communist program. Untold more had died in famines and in the brutal class wars that Mao and the other leaders had periodically stirred. With his blind faith in Marxism, Pol Pot basically agreed with the words of a 1957 speech by Mao: "The Communist Party does not fear criticism because we are Marxists, the truth is on our side, and the basic masses, the workers and peasants, are on our side."[6]

A Rush of Events

While Pol Pot was traveling, two events rocked the Indochinese world. First, the United States introduced three hundred thousand troops into South Vietnam, raising the stakes in its defense of the South Vietnamese government. U.S. planes also began bombing the border region between South Vietnam and Cambodia. Office 100, the Khmer Rouge headquarters, had to be moved north to escape the carnage.

Second, almost a half million suspected Communists were massacred in Indonesia. The massacre was the result of a failed coup attempt, and marked the end of communism in Indonesia. It was easy for the Khmer

Rouge to see parallels with their own situation. The Indonesian president, Sukarno, was flamboyant and unpredictable, like Sihanouk. Also like Sihanouk, he had tried to balance his support between the Communists and non-Communists. It was his military chief, Suharto, who orchestrated the massacre. Again, Suharto recalled the hard-line Cambodian prime minister, Lon Nol. In light of the Indonesian disaster, Pol Pot and the other committee members decided to rethink their approach to Sihanouk's government.

New Tactics

Upon his return from China, Pol Pot called a meeting. The idea of building a temporary alliance with Sihanouk, which had been discussed since the king's embrace of North Vietnam, was rejected now as too risky. Should Lon Nol, who was rabidly anti-Communist, begin to crack down on the Khmer Rouge, Sihanouk would be unable to curb him. Pol Pot urged a more hostile approach to Sihanouk's government.

At the same time, the Cambodian Communists decided to pull back further into obscurity. Office 100 was relocated to Ratanakiri, in the remote forests of north-east Cambodia. The committee also changed the party's name to the Communist Party of Kampuchea (CPK).

In Ratanakiri, Pol Pot and his lieutenants, including Ieng Sary, lived and worked among tribespeople who were far different from the Khmer peasants in their former rural retreats. The tribespeople had grown to hate Sihanouk's government, mainly because of its incursions into their territory. The building of new roads and plantations and the arrival of settlers alarmed them.

Although they also professed to hate the Khmer, the tribespeople forged ties with the Khmer Rouge. In fact, some of their customs became part of the Khmer Rouge's revolutionary program. For example, the tribespeople did not use money and did not trade with groups outside their region. Pol Pot incorporated these ideas into his own rather simplistic notions about economy. The tribes also lacked social classes, which appealed to Pol Pot and the other Marxists. Soon, the Khmer Rouge had enlisted many tribespeople as party members.

During this time, Pol Pot and the committee members made elaborate plans for their future takeover of Cambodia. Maps of the country were divided and redivided into numbered districts. People and resources were shifted around on the maps like pieces in a vast game.

The years the Khmer Rouge spent in the forests of Ratanakiri also gave them a mythic power in the minds of the Cambodian people. Pol Pot's revolutionaries became legendary, like the princes or outlaws in Buddhist and Hindu tales who retired deep into the forests to acquire knowledge and martial fighting skills. Like these heroes, Pol Pot and his followers hoped to return and rout their enemies with almost magical powers.

Uprising in Battambang

Ideas of communism and revolt were already much on the people's minds. In 1967, a peasant uprising broke out in the northwest Cambodian province of Battambang. The cause of the revolt was a brutal crackdown by Lon Nol's soldiers over the illegal sale of rice to the North Vietnamese. Angry peasants stormed some army camps near the village of Samlaut and killed two soldiers. This brought an even more brutal reprisal. Cambodian troops rampaged through the surrounding villages, rounding up suspects and looting indiscriminately.

Sihanouk, just returned from overseas, suspected that Communists in Phnom Penh had incited the peasants. Fearing a loss of authority, he permitted Lon Nol to continue mopping-up operations. Suspected Communists and leftists in Battambang were targeted. Villagers armed with clubs and axes were enlisted to pursue "the Reds." Bounties were offered for the severed heads of Communists. More than one thousand locals died in the violence.

After the uprising, Sihanouk began rounding up Communists in the capital. In a short time, the Communist Party's city-based operations were smashed. Panicked teachers and students with radical sympathies fled to join the guerrilla bands in the countryside.

The episode bore out the worst fears of the Khmer Rouge. As in Indonesia, although on a smaller scale, the government had risen up to virtually eliminate the Communists as a political force. Pol Pot himself nearly died during this time. On foot and weakened by malaria, he traveled for fifteen days to elude Lon Nol's troops. Arriving finally at a remote base, he was nursed back to health by a loyal follower.

The Resistance Grows

The Khmer Rouge changed tactics once again. Somehow they had to take up arms against the Sihanouk government. Rebel bands began to ambush Sihanouk's soldiers and capture their rifles and grenades. In time they built a stockpile of weapons.

News of these skirmishes quickly reached the capital. Despite the recent crackdowns, citizens were losing faith in Sihanouk as a defender against communism. Sihanouk's

During a 1970 televised address, President Richard Nixon announces that American troops have invaded Cambodia in an effort to target Communist bases.

efforts to keep Cambodia out of the Vietnam War were also failing. He reopened diplomatic relations with the United States and allowed U.S. soldiers to pursue the Vietnamese across the border into Cambodia. These acts outraged many students and intellectuals, who hated the United States as another imperial power, and drove them to join the guerrilla movement.

In 1969, Richard M. Nixon took office as president of the United States. With American public opinion turning against the Vietnam War, Nixon was determined

51

to pull U.S. troops out of Vietnam. Before the withdrawal, however, he ordered a secret bombing campaign on Vietnamese Communist bases located near villages inside Cambodia. More than three thousand bombing raids produced huge numbers of casualties. Angered by the relentless attacks on their villages, thousands of Cambodian peasants, both men and women, fled on foot to join the revolution.

A Coup in the Capital

The shift in sentiment weakened Sihanouk's grip on the country. On March 19, 1970, while resting overseas, Sihanouk finally lost control. Lon Nol convinced the National Assembly of Cambodia to remove Sihanouk and had himself declared president. Lon Nol then set about trying to rid Cambodia of the Vietnamese Communists by attacking their bases near the border.

Meanwhile, Sihanouk flew to Beijing for discussions with the Chinese. Zhou Enlai, the Chinese prime minister, advised Sihanouk that the real enemies were Lon Nol and the United States. In his outrage at Lon Nol's treachery, Sihanouk was only too eager to listen to such arguments. The prime minister convinced Sihanouk to lead a coalition that included the Khmer Rouge. Ironically, Pol Pot was in Beijing meeting with the

Chinese at the same time. Sihanouk, however, never learned of his presence. The deposed president still knew nothing about the shadowy leader of the Khmer Rouge.

New Hope for the Revolution

Although still in hiding, Pol Pot realized that events had turned in his favor. With China backing the Khmer Rouge, the North Vietnamese had been forced to recognize the value of Pol Pot's rebels. In fact the two Communist groups, along with Sihanouk, had become allies in the fight against Lon Nol. Now the Khmer Rouge could recruit not only committed radicals but also those who were loyal to Sihanouk. In addition, several hundred Khmer trainees returned from North Vietnam to join the struggle against Lon Nol's government. With about three thousand guerrillas in the hills and forests of Cambodia, the Khmer Rouge finally looked like a fighting force.

The tangle of agreements, alliances, and evasions—what American journalist Elizabeth Becker called "a hall of mirrors"[7]—was as complicated as ever. One fact, however, was clear: Pol Pot's dream of a Communist takeover in Cambodia, which only months before had seemed impossible, now appeared close to coming true.

CHAPTER 4

POL POT COMES TO POWER

As Pol Pot and his colleagues returned to Cambodia on foot, trekking south on the Ho Chi Minh Trail, they were overtaken by trucks hauling military supplies for the North Vietnamese. The North Vietnamese now saw Cambodia as a vital part of their own struggle against South Vietnam and the Americans. They were counting on the Khmer Rouge to help protect their supply lines. In return they offered weapons and strategic aid against Lon Nol's government. The Khmer leaders, and Pol Pot in particular, hated taking orders from the Vietnamese. They recognized, however, that it was necessary, at least for the time being. Once he reached headquarters, Pol Pot sent his old friend Ieng Sary back to Hanoi to coordinate with the Vietnamese.

In April 1970, the United States and the South Vietnamese invaded Cambodia. It was the event that first brought Cambodia to the world's attention. The U.S. objective was to eliminate Vietnamese Communist bases along the border. The invasion inflamed anti-American passions in Cambodia and turned many Americans against the war. Lon Nol, the new prime

Cambodian soldiers watch as U.S. forces bomb Communist areas in the village of O Dar during the 1970 invasion.

minister, was depending on American support in the form of arms and military equipment. His soldiers sought to weed out not only the Vietnamese Communists but also the Khmer Rouge.

Lon Nol's army proved inadequate to the task. Vietnamese Communist forces, with their experience in guerrilla warfare and with help from the Khmer Rouge, began to wear down the government's troops. In late 1971, Lon Nol's depleted forces made one last attempt at a major offensive against the Communists. Its failure marked a turning point in the conflict. With the countryside no longer secure from the Communists, refugees poured into Phnom Penh by the thousands. Basic services soon broke down. Business and trade halted. Stories circulated of brutal acts committed by both sides in the war. The amount of territory that Lon Nol's army controlled was shrinking by the day.

Communist Schools for New Recruits

Faced with the city's collapse, many young people left to join the revolution. New recruits flocked to the guerrillas in every region of the country. The Khmer Rouge no longer feared Lon Nol's agents, and could concentrate now on building the party. Pol Pot and his lieutenants rapidly set up schools for new members.

In 1971, young revolutionaries demonstrate against the government of Lon Nol in the capital city of Phnom Penh.

Recruits listened to the ideas that Pol Pot and the others had developed over the years. They were told that the Khmer Rouge were bringing a national democratic revolution to Cambodia. This revolution was to be distinctly Cambodian in character, relying little on Communist ideas from other countries. No outside help would be needed to seize the country nor to govern it. The fighting prowess of the Khmer Rouge was emphasized, and the North Vietnamese were scarcely mentioned. Above all, the recruits learned that the lower classes were the backbone of the revolution. As one teacher put it, "Farmers and workers must study so as to fall into step with the wheel of history."[8]

Many recruits admired the Khmer Rouge and their attempt to create a new society without the inequities of the past. Others, however, saw signs of a cultlike fervor and a refusal to admit mistakes or adapt ideas to hard realities among Pol Pot's followers. It was not long before their fears were borne out. Khmer Rouge units began taking over villages and giving orders to the people there. Failure to obey often resulted in a fatal bullet.

A Cease-Fire and New Bombing Raids

As the Khmer Rouge grew stronger, the war in Vietnam took another turn. In January 1973, at peace talks in Paris, the North Vietnamese and the United States agreed to a cease-fire. The north withdrew its forces from Cambodia and waited for American troops to leave the region. Secretly, the North Vietnamese planned to make a final assault on South Vietnam once the Americans were gone. North Vietnam urged the Khmer Rouge to honor the cease-fire as well, but Pol Pot refused. He decided that the burgeoning forces of the Khmer Rouge could seize power in Cambodia without

Vietnamese help. His rebel troops continued to ambush units of Lon Nol's scattered army. In response, the United States began massive bombing raids on Khmer Rouge camps and the roads leading to Phnom Penh.

Casualties were staggering, with estimates in the tens of thousands. Further hordes of terrified peasants fled to the cities. Many more joined the Khmer Rouge. The bombing campaign completed the destruction of Cambodian society as it had been. The stage was set for a Communist takeover.

During this time, Sihanouk left Beijing and slipped into Cambodia for meetings with Khmer Rouge leaders. Officials in China and North Vietnam assumed that Sihanouk would still play an important role in Cambodia's future. Pol Pot and the committee members, however, disagreed. They professed allegiance to Sihanouk, but made no promises. Pol Pot amused himself around the former king by posing as a nondescript committee member. Sihanouk did not suspect that this pleasant fellow was actually the notorious leader of the Khmer Rouge.

The Fall of Phnom Penh

By the spring of 1975, the Khmer Rouge were ready to storm the capital. Their ranks had swollen to sixty thousand, including many women and teenagers. Two previous attempts to capture Phnom Penh had failed, mainly because of American bombers. Nevertheless, rebel units controlled all roads into the city. Supplies had to be airlifted in to feed the crowds of refugees. Lon Nol's soldiers had long ceased to be a threat. The U.S. Embassy staff was evacuated by helicopter. Early in April, Lon Nol himself finally fled. The night before Phnom Penh fell, rockets and artillery fire rained down on the city. Thousands tried to escape before the rebels arrived.

On April 17, a viciously hot day in the dry season, the first heavily armed Khmer Rouge troops appeared in the city. A few people emerged to greet them on the street. The troops, some barely in their teens and clad in black pajamas, rejected these overtures with disdain. Guerrillas had been taught to loathe city dwellers as the enemy—untrustworthy ones who refused to fight for the revolution. Dubbed "April 17 people" or "new people," they existed now only to take orders from their conquerors.

There seemed to be little coordinated planning for the actual takeover. People received conflicting messages from different rebel groups. Some were told to remain in their homes and be quiet, while others were ordered to prepare for evacuation. Khmer Rouge soldiers looted shops and flung books from the National Library into the street.

Bursts of automatic weapons fire rang out during the day. Here and there, piles of bloodstained bodies lay on the pavement, a mute warning to those who might disobey.

The Evacuation

Within twenty-four hours, the Khmer Rouge ordered everyone to leave the city. Ostensibly, they were protecting people from possible American bombing attacks. In reality, the evacuation was a display of power and authority. All prior Cambodian history was to be wiped away. Year Zero, the first of the Pol Pot era, had begun.

Those identified as bureaucrats or politicians, or otherwise linked to Lon Nol's regime, were rounded up and shot. Then hundreds of thousands were herded onto the roads and forced to travel on foot in the smothering heat. No one was exempt from the order to march, not even the aged and the crippled. Hospitals were emptied and patients were wheeled along on gurneys, some still with tubes in their arms. Former soldiers—amputees missing feet and legs—shuffled along as best they could. In the confusion, family members were separated, some forever. Deaths from exhaustion or exposure rose into the thousands.

In a matter of days, every city that had been under Lon Nol's control was empty. The evacuees included large numbers of peasants and workers who had fled to the cities to escape the war. Many approved of the Khmer Rouge takeover and sought ways to help them. Pol Pot and the committee, however, showed them no favor. The Communist revolution fed on hatred, and to continue the revolution, that hatred had to be maintained. Professionals, such as doctors, lawyers, engineers, and scientists, were feared for their independent minds and murdered immediately. Even Buddhist monks were killed, and all religious observance strictly banned. Despite his own roots in Buddhism, Pol Pot would allow no authority to challenge that of the new regime. His implacable rebel force soon produced feelings of helplessness in the people. A popular Khmer Rouge slogan illustrates the unimportance of the individual: "To spare you is no profit, to lose you is no loss."[9]

Among the marchers leaving the capital were Pol Pot's brother Loth Suong and his wife. Although they had heard of the mysterious Pol Pot, they did not connect the name to Saloth Sar. It had been twelve years since they had last seen him. As for Pol Pot himself, there is no evidence that he cared what happened to his family members. Another of his brothers, Saloth Chhay, died on the long march.

New prime minister Pol Pot (far left) and other officials are taking office in Phnom Penh.

Putting the Plans into Motion

Seven days after the evacuation began, the leader of the Khmer Rouge secretly entered Phnom Penh. As Pol Pot toured the deserted streets, he reflected on his amazing victory. All who had stood in his way, including the mighty United States, had been vanquished. More than 2 million "enemies of the state" were marching into the countryside to help set up the new Communist system. Nevertheless, Pol Pot was still fearful of surprise attacks and reluctant to be seen in public. For years he had lived as if his enemies were everywhere. It was a habit

63

he could not break. His temporary headquarters was set up in an abandoned railroad station. Khmer Rouge troops ringed the empty city.

At once, Pol Pot and the committee began putting their plans into motion. Until this moment, none of the rank and file had known what to expect. The new program aimed to change every aspect of life in Cambodia.

The Khmer Rouge did away with money, free markets, and private property. They set about reorganizing the nation's most successful asset, its hundreds of farms and rice paddies, into collective farms. April 17 people from the cities, many of whom knew nothing about raising crops, served as slave labor on the farms. People were assigned to tasks with no regard to their training or experience before the revolution. In addition, Pol Pot declared that no foreign aid, including food or medicine, would be allowed into the country. To the outside world, the Cambodian revolution would appear completely independent. In reality, the Khmer Rouge soon accepted aid of more than $1 billion from China, a gift never officially acknowledged.

Building a Government

Pol Pot and his colleagues faced the task of designing a new government for the country. They worked feverishly late into the night, trying to deal with the countless problems of running a state. Papers, reports, lists, memos, proposals, and other documents swelled into enormous piles. It quickly became apparent, however, that none of the Khmer Rouge knew the first thing about running a government. Trained as revolutionaries, they had no skill as economists or administrators. Their proposals, though written in a confident tone, were worthless as public policy. Civil servants, who might have helped them with the most difficult tasks, were instead hacking vines in the countryside.

The nation was renamed Democratic Kampuchea. Pol Pot, the "general secretary," was responsible for the economy and defense. Ieng Sary handled foreign affairs, and Nuon Chea took charge of party business, including education. Officially, the head of state was Norodom Sihanouk. The former king remained a favorite of the Chinese, although Pol Pot and his colleagues considered him only a figurehead. They needed such a front because the Khmer Rouge had yet to reveal their existence to the world.

To create the appearance of a democracy, elections for the national assembly were held. Only soldiers, workers, and peasants could participate. April 17 people could neither run for office nor vote. After the election, Democratic Kampuchea announced to the world the name of its new prime minister—Pol Pot. The first and only act of the national assembly was to approve the new government. It was then dissolved and never mentioned again.

The Four-Year Plan

In 1976, Pol Pot and the committee continued working on the structure of the new government. The result was known as the "Four-Year Plan to Build Socialism in All Fields." The plan embodied Pol Pot's twin goals: to build the country and to defend it. Building the country meant taking charge of its economy, including every aspect of its agriculture, manufacturing, and trade. Defending the country meant purging, or eliminating, every person who might interfere with the committee's plans.

The plan was based on the grandiose schemes of Stalin in Soviet Russia and Mao in China. Each had tried to create a collective economy by force, and the result in each case was failure and massive numbers of deaths. Pol Pot tried to implement his plan with great speed. One reason for this was his long-standing distrust of the Vietnamese. His refusal to follow their instructions in the last years of the Vietnam War had antagonized them. After the revolution, Khmer Rouge troops had instigated skirmishes with the Vietnamese on the border. Pol Pot feared that such confrontations might break out into full-scale war. Before that occurred, he decided, Democratic Kampuchea must have a strong system in place. Also, Pol Pot wanted to institute a socialist system quickly to prevent any revival of capitalism.

Central to the economic plan was the production and sale of rice. Rice production had always been the backbone of Cambodian trade. To Pol Pot, it was even more important because it was the result of peasant labor. The party spread the slogan "three tons of rice per hectare,"[10] a target that was triple the normal yield in Cambodia. To accomplish this, Pol Pot planned to build enormous irrigation projects. Surplus from foreign sales of the rice crop would pay for farm machinery, fertilizers, and insecticides. It would also cover increased defense spending and the building of factories. (How this capital was to be distributed when money had been outlawed in Kampuchea was not explained.) Pol Pot's unyielding belief in communism made him sure that all this was possible.

In reality, few of the party's leaders had any experience in farming. Details about crops and yields eluded them and probably bored them as well. In place of expertise, they offered pie-in-the-sky assurances and revolutionary fervor. Signs of failure, when not blamed on so-called enemies of the state, were met with even more ambitious plans.

Their plans to build heavy industry suffered from the same unreasonable expectations. The Four-Year Plan announced that iron-smelting factories would be built, despite the fact that there were no iron ore deposits in the country. The regime also planned to exploit petroleum and coal resources—if any could be found. No one on the committee would admit to ignorance about these matters.

In place of expertise, the committee offered more slogans. Another slogan coined to inspire the masses was "independence-mastery." Independence reminded the people that they no longer toiled for the French, the Americans, or the Chinese. "Mastery" urged them to accomplish goals undreamed of by past generations or by other countries. To many young Cambodians, it was an appealing message. As the months wore on with little progress, however, their faith began to wane.

Education and Culture

Other changes also shook the people's faith in the revolution. Pol Pot and the Khmer Rouge were determined to control every aspect of life in Democratic Kampuchea. Of course, this included education and cultural events.

These topics occupied only three pages of the Four-Year Plan. To Pol Pot and his colleagues, culture and schooling were not of great importance to the masses. They announced a plan of "half study, half work," but in practice emphasized only the latter. Although their leaders considered themselves intellectuals, the Khmer Rouge all but promoted illiteracy in the people. While there was some primary schooling, no secondary schools were opened until 1978. Books became rare items. From the beginning of the revolution, nonparty intellectuals were suspect, including all those who wore eyeglasses or spoke a foreign language. Eventually such people were summarily shot.

The revolution also tried to wipe away a thousand years of Cambodian culture. With all forms of worship outlawed, the trappings of Hinduism and Buddhism disappeared, including sermons, dramas, and poems. Performances of classical Cambodian dances and music ceased, and radios were banned. The folk culture of the peasants, which was based on family rituals and religious observance, melted away. Everyone wore the same clothes, the black pajamas mandated by the government. Even simple pleasures such as visits to nearby villages or gossiping at dinner were forbidden. The movement of workers was strictly controlled, and they were forced to eat in long dining halls in which everyone sat in regimented silence. In addition, children were separated from their parents and organized into mobile work brigades. Some lucky parents managed to visit their children once every three months.

A Deadly Disagreement

Pol Pot controlled not only the culture and customs of Cambodia, but its history as well. In September 1976, a disagreement over the history of the Communist Party of Kampuchea led to trouble. The party's youth magazine published a story to celebrate what it called the party's twenty-fifth anniversary. This would have placed its beginnings in 1951, when Pol Pot and many of his colleagues were still in Paris.

Pol Pot had always insisted that the party began in 1960, with his participation in the first congress. No alternate versions were allowed. Two longtime party members were arrested as traitors for having spread this error. They were forced to confess and then executed. Increasingly, Pol Pot saw enemies everywhere, and he acted swiftly to eliminate them. The horrors of the Khmer Rouge regime had just begun.

CHAPTER 5

THE KILLING FIELDS

For all of his talk about collectivism, Pol Pot left no doubt that he was the supreme leader of Democratic Kampuchea—or Brother Number One, as the rank and file called him. Yet he soon found that keeping power was as difficult as seizing it had been.

The country was divided into zones, each with its own leadership and its own distinctive problems. Pol Pot suspected that shadowy enemies from these regions coveted his position at the center and were trying to assassinate him. An upset stomach or a bout of fatigue would be labeled a poisoning. No one was above suspicion. Pol Pot made sure that he was never without guards, and he increased the veil of secrecy around party procedures.

To guard against his overthrow, Pol Pot announced a special resolution: "The Authority to Smash [People] Inside and Outside the Ranks." It was, in effect, a license for political murder. Commanders in the various zones could have anyone shot on suspicion of disloyalty. This resulted in waves of purges with no end in sight.

Part of the reason for this paranoia was the regime's sour relations with Vietnam. Raids back and forth across the border fed a mutual distrust. Pol Pot feared that war could break out at any time. Only a strong, united society could withstand the Vietnamese threat. It was only logical to be constantly weeding out those who might weaken the state. Besides, the revolution needed enemies to keep its murderous fervor ablaze.

Interrogation Center S-21

Most party members accused of political crimes were brought to the party's interrogation center S-21. This infamous facility was located in an abandoned high school building in the Phnom Penh suburb of Tuol Sleng. Its director, Kaing Kek Ieu, was a short and spindly former schoolteacher who went by the revolutionary name of Deuch. Deuch had been operating security services for the Khmer Rouge since 1971, when they had first established a safe zone in Cambodia. He believed that all who opposed the regime were traitors and liars. According to a French scholar who was once questioned by Deuch, "He personally beat prisoners who would not tell the 'truth,' a matter which drove him into a rage."[11]

Tuol Sleng Prison employed a staff of more than one hundred guards. These were very young Khmer Rouge recruits, mostly uneducated, aged seventeen to

Tuol Sleng Prison, the notorious Khmer Rouge interrogation center, is now a museum honoring the many victims of Pol Pot.

twenty-one. Many of them had known nothing but warfare their whole lives. The few prisoners who survived Tuol Sleng invariably remarked on their stone-faced viciousness.

The center contained all the earmarks of a bureaucracy: typists, scribes, file clerks, and photographers. Prisoners were brought to the center, photographed, interrogated (sometimes in several sessions), and then executed, usually by a shot to the head. Deuch and the other interrogators routinely beat the prisoners, demanding that they confess to various crimes, such as spying for the Vietnamese or for the U.S. Central Intelligence Agency. Most of the charges were absurd, but the prisoners would confess to almost anything in the hope that the torture would end.

Confessions were handwritten, or, if especially interesting, typed with several carbons. Clerks carefully filed the confessions, and tried to cross-reference the information they contained. To satisfy their superiors, the staff at Tuol Sleng constantly found more and more evidence of spying and treason. Their work fed Pol Pot's paranoia, which ensured that the flow of prisoners only increased. Workers in the neighborhood of Tuol Sleng began calling it "the place where people went in and never came out."[12]

TUOL SLENG PRISON

The Khmer Rouge's most notorious prison was its Security Office 21 at a former high school at Tuol Sleng. In the Khmer language, Tuol Sleng means "hill of the poisonous tree" or "hill of guilt." The facility housed those identified as enemies of the regime. These prisoners were systematically questioned and put to death.

New prisoners were first photographed and then stripped of all possessions. In the cells, they were shackled to the floor or wall. What sleep they could get was done on the floor without benefit of blankets or mats. They were required to ask the guards' permission for everything, even relieving themselves. Acting without permission resulted in a severe beating.

A poster on the wall of each cell informed prisoners of the rules at Tuol Sleng. According to the Web site Cambodian Communities Out of Crisis, these included:

- You must immediately answer my questions without wasting time to reflect.
- While getting lashes or electrification you must not cry at all.
- Do nothing. Sit still and wait for my orders. If there is no order, keep quiet. When I ask you to do something, you must do it right away without protesting.
- If you do not follow all of the above rules, you shall get many lashes of electric wire.
- If you disobey any point of my regulations, you shall get either ten lashes or five shocks of electric discharge.

This young girl was one of thousands murdered at S-21. Her photo hangs on a wall at the museum.

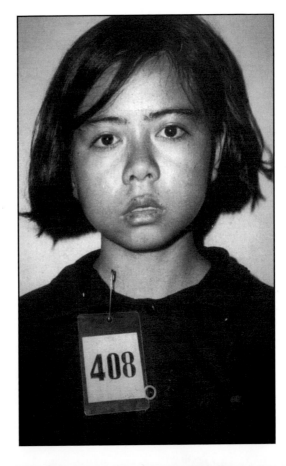

Purging the Party Faithful

In late 1976, the number of arrests skyrocketed. The prisoners included longtime party members and friends of Pol Pot. Often, even the wives and children of the accused were imprisoned.

Typical were two party leaders named Keo Meas and Ney Saran. Meas had begun his revolutionary career in the 1950s. He had traveled with Pol Pot to Vietnam and China, and considered the leader (whom he called Pouk) a close friend. Saran had similar ties to Brother Number One, including years working together at a Khmer Rouge outpost. Arrested on trumped-up charges of treason, both men were brutally tortured and put to death. In the notes of his so-called confession, Meas maintained that he was a loyal Khmer and wondered why his old friend had abandoned him. The whole procedure seemed to perplex him.

As for Pol Pot, he disdained any feelings for his victims. To him, they were as insignificant as germs. He even referred to them as microbes. It was the duty of the revolution to root them out and eliminate them. He emphasized this duty in his speeches to small groups of party members, and calmly noted how each person squirmed.

By mid-1977, the purges had an unstoppable momentum. The interrogation center at Tuol Sleng had to add tape recorders and an improved filing system to handle all the prisoners. Now the relatives and friends of accused party members were being hauled in. As a result, those in the revolution who were intelligent and had some talent—and thus were more apt to express a personal opinion or original idea—were steadily disappearing.

Genocide of Non-Khmers

Also disappearing at an alarming rate were people not of Pol Pot's approved racial makeup. Generally this included all those who were not ethnic Khmer peasants, whom Pol Pot saw as the heart of the revolution. The purges sought to wipe out so-called enemies of the state. Usually these enemies were identified in class terms, but race played a large role as well.

The Vietnamese were just one of the many groups targeted. Others included ethnic Thais, Chinese, and Cham Muslims. Following any custom that the Khmer leaders considered foreign was strictly forbidden. For example, a Muslim family that refused to eat pork in the standard meals provided them would be executed at once. A Chinese worker might be shot for uttering a phrase in his native language. The best hope for a member of an ethnic minority was to claim to be very poor—and thus part of the proletariat that Pol Pot championed.

The death toll among ethnic groups was staggering. Almost 50 percent of the ethnic Chinese in Cambodia—more than two hundred thousand people—perished during the Pol Pot regime. Half the population of Cham Muslims was also murdered.

The Killing Fields

Murder was, in fact, the leading industry of the Khmer Rouge regime. Most of the killings took place in the countryside, usually at sunset. The country had become a gigantic prison farm, and the murders served to keep the workers frightened and obedient. Often a wave of murders would follow the rice-planting season, to weed out those considered parasites by the regime. Workers in the rice paddies began referring to "the killing fields"— the secluded sites of so many murders. Typical is this account by Darith Keo, who was raised in Battambang and was a child during the Pol Pot era:

Each day as we toiled in rice fields we saw men and women with hands tied behind their backs being led away by soldiers. Each time I saw this my heart would race. Before my heartbeat could return to normal I would hear gunshots echoing in the background. Sometimes the soldiers were not so discreet. Once they made the people sit in a circle and watch as they executed an unmarried couple. They were clubbed on the neck and fell near a ditch. The Khmer Rouge henchmen pushed them into the hole with their shins.[13]

War Breaks Out with Vietnam

While the killings proceeded inside Cambodia, Pol Pot and a few colleagues visited their fellow Communist leaders in China and North Korea. In Beijing, Pol Pot paid tribute to Mao, who had died a short time before, and pledged his support for Mao's ideas of continuous revolution. In private talks, he urged the Chinese to support his regime against the Vietnamese. During his stay in China, a prerecorded speech was broadcast on Radio Phnom Penh in which he finally announced to the world the existence of the Communist Party of Kampuchea.

In North Korea, as in China, the leader of the Khmer Rouge was welcomed and praised. The North Koreans broadcast a brief biography of Pol Pol that sketched his revolutionary past. In keeping with his preference for secrecy, this program was not aired in the Khmer language for home consumption.

Late in 1977, Pol Pot returned to find his regime at war with the Vietnamese. After months of border skirmishes, Vietnam had finally launched a full-scale attack. It was timed to show Vietnam's displeasure with Pol Pot's trip to China. After only a few weeks of fighting, however, the Vietnamese withdrew their forces. Pol Pot claimed a great victory for the Khmer Rouge. Khmer units continued to make raids across the border, slaughtering Vietnamese villagers and burning their homes. Angry Vietnamese leaders bided their time for another offensive.

Purge in the Eastern Zone

Should the fighting with Vietnam intensify, the Khmer Rouge would need help from friendly nations. With this in mind, Pol Pot made a few cosmetic changes to the regime to improve its image to world leaders. He welcomed visitors, both state officials and media members, from various pro-Chinese Communist parties. The visitors were taken to specially prepared sites to witness the progress made in agriculture and the peasants' standards of living. To demonstrate his regime's openness, Pol Pot freed some April 17 people and some Cambodians who had innocently returned to the country after being educated overseas. (The first wave of these expatriates, particularly those who had studied in the United States, had been executed immediately upon their return.)

Elsewhere, however, the regime continued its war with itself. In the Eastern Zone, where Vietnamese troops had penetrated farthest, a vicious purge ripped through the Khmer Rouge military to punish supposed treachery and incompetence. An estimated one hundred

In 1977, Deng Xiao-Ping (right), a top Communist official of China, shakes hands with Pol Pot (center) in Beijing.

thousand soldiers and party members, along with their families, were rounded up and murdered. Troops in the northeast were also purged. In both zones, hundreds of thousands of people were forced to move away from the border to avoid capture by the Vietnamese. The grueling marches resulted in many more deaths from exhaustion and exposure.

Pol Pot's virtual war with the Eastern Zone represented a break with his own past. It was there that he had hidden in forest camps and nursed plans for the revolution. The eastern leaders were longtime friends and colleagues from the Office 100 days. He had also depended on the border people, both Cambodian and Vietnamese, for support in those lean years. Now all of them were feeling his fury. No other region in the country was dealt with as harshly as the east.

The Cult of the Leader

As Pol Pot's paranoia grew, so did his insistence on his position as supreme leader. In the confessions at Tuol Sleng, Pol Pot was referred to in awestruck tones as "the party center" or "the organization" (*angkar* in the Khmer language). His habits of seclusion only added to his stature among the rank and file. In their minds, they connected him to the legendary heroes of Cambodian

This pile of skulls at a memorial site serves as a grim reminder of the Khmer Rouge's campaign of genocide against the Cambodian people.

folklore who slew powerful enemies through magic and cunning. Pol Pot's victories over Lon Nol and his American supporters would not soon be forgotten by Cambodians who had never before known independence.

Pol Pot came close to establishing a "cult of personality" in Cambodia. This is when one leader becomes synonymous with a state or revolution, as Mao did in China and Stalin did in the Soviet Union. As evidence of such a cult, paintings and statues of Pol Pot began to appear throughout the nation, some created by prisoners at Tuol Sleng. Huge photographs of the leader were

83

hung in the dining halls on the collective farms. In fact, it was the sight of one of these photographs that made Loth Suong realize that the all-powerful Pol Pot was actually his long-lost brother Saloth Sar.

A National Party Congress

Pol Pot's sway over the party was on display in a national congress held in September 1978. The meeting coincided with celebrations of the party's anniversary. In a speech at the Olympic Stadium, Pol Pot ran through all the old themes. He assured his audience that the Vietnamese were no real threat to Democratic Kampuchea, that collectivism in the country had been a huge success, and that an overwhelming majority of the people believed in the party's goals. As usual, he spoke simply and modestly, like a Buddhist teacher or like a father speaking to his children.

Whether or not his listeners believed him, the evidence all around them disputed their leader's words. In the Eastern Zone, the purges were raging even as Vietnamese planes renewed attacks on Khmer units. Hapless young Khmer recruits struggled to learn how to use Chinese mortars and tanks. Meanwhile, just across the border with Vietnam, Cambodians opposed to the regime were beginning to organize.

Opposition in the East

Since the summer of 1978, thousands of anti–Khmer Rouge fighters had joined forces to make sneak attacks against the regime. Heng Samrin, a veteran party member from the east, led the resistance. Samrin had commanded units that seized Phnom Penh back in 1975. Now, completely disillusioned with the Khmer Rouge program, Samrin and his associates hoped to topple Pol Pot and liberate the country. The Vietnamese pledged support to Samrin and his United Front for the National Salvation of Kampuchea.

When Pol Pot's troops in the Eastern Zone attacked Samrin's forces, the rebel leader pulled back into Vietnam. More than ten thousand Cambodian refugees followed him. Late in 1978 Samrin resumed his guerrilla attacks. When an area was liberated, he and his rebels would immediately abolish the most hateful of the Khmer Rouge laws. He brought in monks to speak to the people, showing his tolerance for religion. Soon, the United Front had gained a base of popular support. With the help of the Vietnamese, they soon launched a wider offensive.

CHAPTER 6

POL POT IN EXILE

$\mathscr{I}$n spite of his paranoia about plots and assassins, Pol Pot allowed several foreign journalists to visit Democratic Kampuchea and interview him in December 1978. Two Americans, Elizabeth Becker and Richard Dudman, became the first writers from a nonsocialist country to question the Khmer Rouge leader. Accompanying them was a radical professor from London named Malcolm Caldwell, who had praised the Cambodian revolution from the beginning.

Becker and Dudman had to submit their questions before the interview. They were ushered into a huge room at one end of which sat Pol

Pot, framed by floor-to-ceiling windows. Becker described him as "elegant—with a pleasing smile and delicate, alert eyes."[14] His high-collared gray suit was in the style of Mao. Pol Pot greeted the journalists without rising, then proceeded to lecture them for more than an hour. He claimed to want peace and painted the Vietnamese as the true threat in the region. As Becker put it: "He ranted and raved about the impending Vietnamese invasion—always in the quietest of tones."[15] She left the meeting convinced that Pol Pot was insane.

Despite constant fears for his safety, Pol Pot grants an interview to two American journalists in Cambodia in 1978.

Norodom Sihanouk addresses the United Nations Security Council after the Vietnamese invasion of Cambodia in 1979.

Subsequent events only added to her dismay. Caldwell was able to meet with Pol Pot alone because of the admiring articles he had written about the regime in the past. After his chat, Caldwell told Becker that he had been delighted with Pol Pot's honesty and was convinced that the Cambodian revolution had been worthwhile.

Around midnight, in a guesthouse for visitors, Becker was awakened by the sound of gunshots from Caldwell's room. She ran into the hallway, where a man with bandoliers of bullets on his chest nearly knocked her down. He pointed his pistol at her, but she escaped into a bathroom. Caldwell had been shot and killed. Some claimed that a party faction opposed to Pol Pot was hoping that Caldwell's murder would embarrass the leader in the world press. Others blamed the murder on Pol Pot himself.

The Vietnamese Invasion

News of Caldwell's death was quickly overshadowed by the next day's events. More than one hundred thousand Vietnamese troops, joined by fifteen thousand Cambodian rebels, launched an attack across the Cambodian border. Vietnamese fighter planes provided cover for the invasion. The operation, called Blooming Lotus, was designed to strike at the center of Cambodia and then fan out to destroy the surrounding command posts.

Combat was fierce, but the experienced Vietnamese were able to outmaneuver the Khmer units. Within a week, on January 1, 1979, Vietnamese troops controlled large swaths of territory in the east and were relentlessly moving toward the capital. The thunder of artillery rattled the windows of Pol Pot's headquarters in Phnom Penh.

The attack was Pol Pot's worst nightmare. At once, he claimed that the Soviets and nations under Soviet influence were helping the Vietnamese. He refused to admit that his hated enemies had the upper hand. He even predicted to a delegation from Canada that Vietnam would soon be defeated.

Pol Pot Goes into Exile

Despite his brave words, Pol Pot realized that his regime was in grave danger. Purges of military leaders and troops in the Eastern Zone not only had weakened Cambodian defenses, they had also driven thousands of disgusted Khmer Rouge into the hands of the Vietnamese. Pol Pot cast about desperately for a tactical weapon. Finally, he settled on the former king, Norodom Sihanouk.

When the Khmer Rouge had seized power in 1975, they had made Sihanouk the ceremonial head of state. Sihanouk still had support from China and its prime minister, Zhou Enlai, and he presented a reassuring face to the outside world. In 1976, after Zhou's death, Sihanouk had been removed from office and placed under house arrest in Phnom Penh. There he had remained until now.

At a hastily arranged meeting, Sihanouk joined Pol Pot to sip orange juice and discuss the situation. The two leaders spoke politely about the past, and Sihanouk was charmed to be called "Your Highness." Pol Pot even apologized for having failed to meet with Sihanouk since the Khmer Rouge takeover.

Pol Pot urged Sihanouk to travel to the United Nations and explain his country's desperate need for help. He also sketched the military situation for the former king, assuring him that the Vietnamese could be defeated

LAND MINES IN CAMBODIA

A frequent reminder of the horrors of the Pol Pot regime in Cambodia is an exploding land mine. Thousands of the mines are still buried throughout the country, particularly in the northwest and in the border regions next to Thailand.

The Khmer Rouge and other members of the antigovernment coalition planted the mines in rice fields, along paths, and on the outskirts of villages. Generally even the soldiers who laid the mines did not make maps of where they are. No thought was given to the effects of the devices after the war.

Each mine is about the size of an apple and is buried no more than an inch or two below the ground. A mine is activated by the pressure of someone's foot or the weight of a tire. The victim hears a loud click just before the explosion. More than two thousand people each year are killed or maimed by land mines in Cambodia. Perhaps fifty thousand Cambodians have lost a limb due to an exploding mine.

Experts estimate that as many as 4 to 6 million mines are still buried in the Cambodian soil. International groups have raised money to find and disable the mines, but much more needs to be done. The problem has helped to discourage tourism, as well. Red signs warning about minefields dot the countryside. Tourists in remote areas are advised to use the Khmer phrase "*Mian min dtay?*" (Are there mines here?)

Children play near a sign warning of the danger posed by hidden land mines, a legacy of the Khmer Rouge.

in a matter of months. Sihanouk agreed to undertake the mission. When he returned to his home that night, his wife was astonished that he had not been shot.

Events outraced Pol Pot's schemes to save his government. Soon, the Vietnamese had the capital surrounded with five divisions. Sihanouk's flight was the last to leave Phnom Penh before the Vietnamese arrived. Diplomats from many other nations also were on board, having judged that a Vietnamese victory was inevitable. Hundreds of government workers scrambled to escape the city by train. In the chaos, two helicopters rose above Phnom Penh and sliced off toward the horizon. Their passengers included Pol Pot and his last trusted colleagues. The Khmer Rouge regime had come to an end.

A New Cambodian Government

The government that replaced the Khmer Rouge in Cambodia consisted of former party members who had fled to Vietnam and other Khmer who had lived in exile there for twenty years. The Vietnamese installed the new government, called the People's Republic of Kampuchea, as a satellite state with Heng Samrin as president. Up to two hundred thousand Vietnamese troops remained to keep order. Vietnam's leaders planned to control Cambodia virtually as a colony and thus ensure that Pol Pot did not return. Most Cambodians accepted the first condition with reluctance, but heartily supported the second.

The new government, while still run by Communists, hastily abolished many of the worst features of Pol Pot's rule. Money and markets were restored, schools and hospitals reopened, families reunited, and travel restrictions eased. Worship in the Buddhist faith was not encouraged, but it was tolerated. Those who could no longer abide Marxism-Leninism in any form left for Thailand.

When the tide turned, Khmer Rouge troops had retreated into the forests along the border with Thailand. Thousands had fallen in combat, and thousands more died from malaria and starvation. Some of Pol Pot's soldiers were captured and lynched by angry villagers. Even when captured, the Khmer Rouge remained defiant. They promised the people that they would escape and "turn the population into fish paste."[16]

With Pol Pot's departure, many Cambodian refugees decided to return. Millions took to the roads, searching for lost family members and the remains of villages. Jails were emptied, and political prisoners were freed. Mobs broke into warehouses to retrieve items of modern life, such as bicycles and radios, that the Khmer Rouge had forbidden. The entire country was like a groggy sleeper awakening from a nightmare.

Exile in Thailand

The architect of that nightmare was not far away. Pol Pot took up residence in a series of fortified camps on the Thai border. Now and then he and his colleagues would slip into Cambodia for a short time, but then withdraw for fear of being captured. Pol Pot's intent was to rebuild the Khmer Rouge military and retake Cambodia.

Governments hostile to Vietnam, including those of Thailand, China, and the United States, protected the former dictator. Following their lead, the United Nations recognized Pol Pot's regime as a government-in-exile. The Khmer Rouge were allowed to keep their country's seat at the United Nations. This state of affairs became embarrassing as reporters and historians began to investigate the brief history of Democratic Kampuchea. What they discovered about events there in the preceding four years shocked the world.

The Truth About the Khmer Rouge

One of the first writers who shone a light on Pol Pot's regime was a French missionary named François Ponchaud. Shortly after the fall of Phnom Penh,

Ponchaud published *Cambodia: Year Zero*. The book detailed the Cambodian catastrophe, from the evacuation of the cities to the slave labor farms to the senseless killings. At first, Communist supporters worldwide tried to discredit the book's claims. As more accounts were published, however, the truth could no longer be ignored or denied. Pol Pot had presided over a regime that rivaled the worst of the twentieth century in its policies of death and destruction.

The raw numbers were staggering. In the three years, eight months, and twenty days that the Khmer Rouge ruled in Cambodia, more than 1.5 million men, women,

At Tuol Sleng Prison, French tourists look at a map of Cambodia formed from the skulls and bones of some of Pol Pot's victims.

and children were murdered or otherwise lost their lives. That total represented one-quarter of the population. An additional five hundred thousand refugees had escaped to Thailand and Vietnam.

In 1979, the new government turned Tuol Sleng Prison into the Genocide Museum as a tribute to Pol Pot's victims. Officials found mass graves and dug up the remains of slain prisoners. A towering stack of skulls became a symbol of the regime's terrible abuses. Historians began to pore through thousands of pages of confessions. The prisoners' frightened words verified the worst about the former leader's paranoia and cold calculation.

In scattered interviews, Pol Pot insisted that only a few hundred or a few thousand people had actually lost their lives during his years of leadership. He also claimed that the regime's harsh measures were necessary to prevent the Vietnamese from seizing Cambodia. Those who had "Cambodian bodies and Vietnamese minds"[17] had to be eliminated to save the revolution.

As the truth about the Khmer Rouge emerged, Pol Pot came to rival Hitler and Stalin as an emblem of a murderous despot. The new government in Cambodia placed Pol Pot and Ieng Sary on trial in absentia. The result was a guilty verdict and a death sentence that could not be enforced. The International Court of Justice hoped to try Pol Pot as well, but the Thai government refused to turn him over. In this, it was supported by the United States and China.

A Coalition Government

Revelations about Pol Pot's history caused the United States to put together a coalition to replace the Khmer Rouge as government-in-exile. Their seat at the United Nations had become a particular embarrassment. The new coalition was made up of three factions. Two of the factions were non-Communist: Norodom Sihanouk led one, and a former prime minister, Son Sann, led another. The third faction was made up of officials from the former Democratic Kampuchea. Khieu Samphan, Pol Pot's lieutenant, served as the coalition's spokesperson. Samphan made a show of his conversion to capitalist ideas and also claimed that his work for the Khmer Rouge had not been voluntary. In reality, Samphan had been involved in the purges from the start.

The factions, with their mutual dislike of each other, formed a coalition in name only. Little was changed in practice. Pol Pot continued to rebuild Khmer forces and launch brief raids across the border. Weapons for coalition forces came from the Chinese, while the

Americans and Thais gave money to the non-Communist factions only.

Going Underground

In spite of foreign aid given to Khmer troops, Pol Pot failed to assemble a force that could successfully invade Cambodia. In fact, for the next five years, he mostly remained in the shadows of Indochinese affairs, a wild card in the pack, never quite forgotten. With one notable exception, no speeches, articles, or photographs emerged from the former leader. Nonetheless, Cambodians who had lived through the horrors of the Khmer Rouge regime dreaded the possibility of his return.

The exception to his silence was a speech to party members that he delivered in 1981. From reports, it seems to be the only instance in which Pol Pot showed remorse for his deeds. According to an anonymous witness:

> He said that he knows that many people in the country hate him and think he's responsible for the killings. He said that he knows many people died. When he said this he nearly broke down and cried. He said he must accept responsibility because the line was too far to the left, and because he didn't keep proper track of what was going on.[18]

Secluded in his fortified camp, Pol Pot knew little about events in the wider world. His focus on restoring the revolution never ceased. Privately, he married a second wife, a peasant girl much younger than he, and had a daughter with her. His first wife, Khieu Ponnary, had been hospitalized in the early 1980s and was rumored to have gone mad.

Later in the decade, a curious document was obtained by the U.S. Embassy in Bangkok, Thailand. In it, Pol Pot reflected on his short-lived regime and compared it to others in recent history. He declared that there had been victories, such as the Four-Year Plan, and mistakes—none of which he linked to any person. In the history of the world, he pointed out, there had never been a country that avoided making mistakes.

Grandfather 87

In his last years, Pol Pot had ample time to reflect on his mistakes. He continued to live in seclusion, within double barbed-wire fences surrounding a spartan compound named Office 87. Pol Pot's own Cambodian bodyguards were backed up by Thai troops who monitored all visitors.

Vietnam finally withdrew from Cambodia in 1989. Pol Pot refused to participate in the peace agreement that installed a non-Communist government. By this

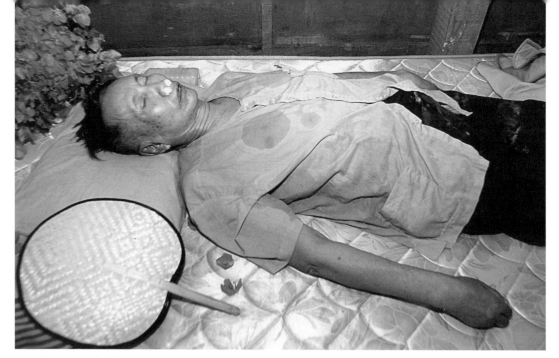

In 1998, the lifeless body of Pol Pot lies on a bed in a small hut near the Thai border.

time, he had officially retired as head of the Khmer Rouge, although he continued to plan strategy with the leadership. Oddly enough, his faction had amassed a fortune of more than $100 million from mining and timber interests, freeing it from the need for foreign aid. The money, however, did nothing to increase the group's effectiveness.

As events left him behind, Pol Pot returned to an activity that had always appealed to him—teaching. Students would brave the frontier to sit at his feet as if he were a Buddhist master. Grandfather 87, as they called him, never stopped predicting that the Khmer Rouge would return to power. To him, the world had scarcely changed since the 1950s.

The Death of Pol Pot

Party members and troops were not as immune to world events. By the middle 1990s, many Khmer Rouge were drifting away. A splinter group of moderates left to join the new government, while the more hard-line members stayed with Pol Pot.

In 1997, even these members finally turned on the leader after a bloody struggle for power. Pol Pot, in a return to his dictatorial ways, ordered the execution of his longtime friend Son Sen, the Khmer defense minister, as well as Sen's wife and nine children. The leader of the hard-line Khmer Rouge faction, General Ta Mok, seized the aged Pol Pot and put him on trial for his many crimes. The Khmer Rouge sentenced Pol Pot to lifelong house arrest. By this time, rumors of his failing health began to reach the West.

Seizing on the rebels' weakness, Cambodian government troops attempted to wipe out the remainder of the Khmer Rouge and eliminate them as a threat. Mok escaped to the mountains with Pol Pot to evade government forces. Mok hoped eventually to use the former leader as a bargaining chip to save his fellow Khmer Rouge. There was talk of handing Pol Pot over to an international tribunal for a public trial. On April 15, 1998, however, Pol Pot died, apparently of a heart attack, in a small hut beside the Thai border in northern Cambodia.

Legacy of a Tyrant

Saloth Sar's rise to power as the tyrant Pol Pot was a catastrophe for Cambodia. His radical policies tore apart families, created thousands of refugees, and left more than a million dead. As a committed Marxist, he claimed to want to improve the lives of the poorest peasants. Instead, he and the Khmer Rouge treated the people like work animals and snatched away what few pleasures they had. His dream of an independent Cambodia was shared by many of his countrymen. His program for achieving it, however, was a miserable failure.

Today, Cambodia is one of the world's poorest nations. Its standards of health and education lag far behind those of most other countries in Asia. Factions still struggle to form a united government. While the war has ended, violent crime and corruption continue to plague the people.

The Khmer Rouge no longer exist. Of the remaining leaders, some were convicted of their crimes and some were pardoned. Many former Khmer Rouge have joined the new government.

That the son of a peasant farmer could rise to become the supreme leader of Cambodia is extraordinary. Yet Pol Pot's legacy is one of inept rule and mass murder. His country is still trying to overcome the effects of this legacy.

CHRONOLOGY

May 25, 1928	Saloth Sar, the future Pol Pot, is born in a village north of Phnom Penh.
1935	Sar goes to a Catholic primary school in Phnom Penh.
1942	Sar enters an elite boarding school.
1949	Sar sails to France to study on scholarship.
1952	Sar returns to Cambodia as a member of the Communist Party. He begins underground work in his home country under various names, including Pol.
1953	France grants independence to Cambodia.
1955	The Geneva agreement creates a divided Vietnam. Norodom Sihanouk's party sweeps the Cambodian elections.
1956	Pol Pot begins a career as a teacher, and marries another teacher, Khieu Ponnary.

1960	A party congress of the Communist Party of Kampuchea is held. Pol Pot is named to the party's central committee.
1963	Pol Pot's original name appears on a government list of suspected Communists. He goes into hiding as a Communist revolutionary.
1963–1970	Pol Pot works in secret for the revolution.
1970	Sihanouk is replaced by Lon Nol as leader of Cambodia.
1973	U.S. bombers strike the Khmer Rouge.
1975	The Khmer Rouge seize the government of Cambodia. The country is renamed Democratic Kampuchea. Cities are evacuated and collective farms are established.
1976	Pol Pot becomes prime minister of Democratic Kampuchea.
1978	War breaks out with a major Vietnamese attack on Cambodia.
1979	Vietnam defeats the Khmer Rouge and establishes a puppet regime. Pol Pot and his top colleagues flee to the Thailand border.

1980–1992	Pol Pot plans a return to power as one faction in an antigovernment coalition.
1995	Members of the Khmer Rouge are captured or leave to join the new government.
April 15, 1998	Pol Pot dies of an apparent heart attack.

GLOSSARY

class warfare The idea that the lower or working classes should be in conflict with the upper or wealthy classes.

collective farm A government-run farm on which workers pool their labor.

communism An economic and political system in which there is no private property and no social classes.

Democratic Kampuchea The name given to Cambodia by the Khmer Rouge government.

expatriate A person who is living outside his or her home country.

genocide The systematic attempt to wipe out an entire ethnic group.

Indochina A linked group of three countries in Southeast Asia—Cambodia, Laos, and Vietnam—that were once under French control.

indoctrinate Convince others to accept or believe a system of ideas.

Khmer Rouge (Literally, "Red Khmer") The name given to the Communist Party of Kampuchea.

Marxist A person who follows the ideas of Karl Marx, the first proponent of communism.

proletariat Working people.

propaganda Information and stories that are slanted toward one point of view.

purge A movement to eliminate those who oppose a government or a leader.

radical Politically in favor of revolutionary ideas.

satellite state A country that is completely controlled by another country.

tribunal A court for trying offenders.

Tuol Sleng A former high school in Phnom Penh that was used as a prison by the Khmer Rouge.

united front A group of factions that have joined together to oppose a government.

Vietminh North Vietnamese guerrilla fighters.

SOURCE NOTES

Chapter 1: The Original Khmer

1. Quoted in David P. Chandler, *Brother Number One: A Political Biography of Pol Pot.* Boulder, CO: Westview Press, 1999, p. 9.

2. Quoted in Chandler, *Brother Number One*, p. 39.

Chapter 2: Apprentice to Communism

3. Quoted in Ben Kiernan, *How Pol Pot Came to Power: Colonialism, Nationalism, and Communism in Cambodia, 1930–1975.* New Haven, CT: Yale University Press, 2004, p. 45.

4. Quoted in Chandler, *Brother Number One*, p. 66.

Chapter 3: The Khmer Rouge

5. Quoted in Kiernan, *How Pol Pot Came to Power*, p. 218.

6. Quoted in "A Biography of Mao Tse-tung," www.geocities.com/franith.

7. Quoted in Chandler, *Brother Number One*, p. 91.

Chapter 4: Pol Pot Comes to Power

8. Quoted in Chandler, *Brother Number One*, p. 96.

9. Quoted in "Talking About Genocide," The Peace Pledge Union, www.ppu.org.uk/genocide/g_cambodia1.html.

10. Quoted in Chandler, *Brother Number One*, p. 123.

Chapter 5: The Killing Fields

11. Quoted in Ben Kiernan, *The Pol Pot Regime: Race, Power, and Genocide in Cambodia Under the Khmer Rouge, 1975–79.* New Haven, CT: Yale University Press, 2002, p. 315.

12. Quoted in Chandler, *Brother Number One*, p. 133.

13. Dith Pran, compiler, *Children of Cambodia's Killing Fields: Memoirs by Survivors.* New Haven, CT: Yale University Press, 1997, p. 164.

Chapter 6: Pol Pot in Exile

14. Quoted in Elizabeth Becker, "Pol Pot Remembered," BBC Online, April 20, 1998. http://news.bbc.co.uk/1/hi/world/from_our_own_corr espondent/81048.stm.

15. Quoted in Becker, "Pol Pot Remembered."

16. Quoted in Kiernan, *The Pol Pot Regime*, p. 454.

17. Quoted in Chandler, *Brother Number One*, p. 168.

18. Quoted in Chandler, *Brother Number One*, p. 171.

For More Information

Books

Robert Green, *Cambodia*. San Diego, CA: Lucent Books, 2003.

Andy Koopmans, *Pol Pot*. San Diego, CA: Lucent Books, 2005.

Dith Pran, compiler, *Children of Cambodia's Killing Fields: Memoirs by Survivors*. New Haven, CT: Yale University Press, 1997.

Web Sites

Cambodia: Beauty and Darkness (www.mekong.net/cambodia). A useful general site about Cambodia, with a detailed history, oral histories, maps, photos, and articles about Cambodian culture.

Cambodia Information Center (www.cambodia.org). An English-language Cambodian site that is devoted to history, culture, and current events in the country.

INDEX

April 17 people, 60, 64, 65, 80

Battambang (Cambodia), 49–50
Becker, Elizabeth, 53, 86–89
Beijing (China), 44–46
Blooming Lotus, 89
bombing raids, 46, 52, 59
Brother Number One, 39, 71, 76
Buddhism, 14, 16, 69, 93

Caldwell, Malcolm, 86–89
Cambodia
    China and, 30
    Democratic Party, 17–18
    education and culture in, 68, 70
    elections in, 29
    foreign aid and, 64
    France and, 12–14, 16–17, 26
    Geneva Settlement and, 27–29
    geography of, 11
    history of, 7–8, 10, 12–14
    revolution in, 21, 39
    U.S. bombing raids and, 59
    Vietnam and, 30, 55, 58–59, 89, 92–93, 99
    see also Democratic Kampuchea
Cambodia: Year Zero (Ponchaud), 95
Cambodian Communists, 43, 47, 70
capitalism, 19, 67
cease-fire, 58
Chea, Nuon, 36, 37, 65
children, 69–70
China, 7, 66, 94
    Cambodia and, 30, 64
    Communist revolution in, 44
    Khmer Rouge and, 53, 79

    support for Sihanouk and, 90
coalition government, 97–98
collectivism, 20, 64, 71, 84
communism, 18–21, 24–39, 46–47
Communist Manifesto, The (Marx and Engels), 19
Communist Party, 36–37, 42, 43, 47, 70
Communist Party of Kampuchea (CPK), 47–48, 79
concentration camps, 20
cult of personality, 82–84

Democratic Kampuchea, 5, 65, 97
Democratic Party, 17–18, 29, 31
Deuch, 72–73, 74
Duan, Le, 43–44
Dudman, Richard, 86–89

Eastern Zone, 80–82, 84, 90
Engels, Friedrich, 19
ethnic minorities, 77–78

First Indochina War, 28
foreign aid, 64
Four-Year Plan, 66–68, 99
France, 7, 12–14, 16–17, 26, 29, 42
French Communist Party, 23, 24–25

Geneva Settlement, 27–29
genocide, 77–78
Genocide Museum, 96
government-in-exile, 94, 97
Grandfather 87, 100
guerrillas, 25, 42, 53, 56, 60, 85

Ho Chi Minh, 28

Ieu, Kaing Kek, 72–73
Indochina Communist Party (ICP), 24–25
interrogation center S-21, 72–74, 75

Khmer, 13, 22, 30
Khmer Rouge, 5, 6, 8, 40–53, 79
    ambush Sihanouk's soldiers, 50
    backed by China, 53
    builds Vietnamese Communist Party, 56
    end of, 92–94
    as government-in-exile, 97–98
    murders by, 9, 78–79, 95–96
    North Vietnam and, 43, 54
    Phnom Penh and, 59–62
    purges by, 80–82
    takes over Cambodia, 8–9, 64
    truth about, 94–97
    Vietminh and, 41–42
    war with Vietnam and, 79–80, 84
killing fields, 71–85

Laos, 7, 11, 12
land mines, 91
Lenin, Vladimir, 19–20
Little Red Book (Mao Tse-tung), 45
Livre Noir (Pol Pot), 43–44

Mao Tse-tung, 44, 45, 66, 79, 83
Marx, Karl, 19
Marxism, 19, 46, 48, 102
Meas, Keo, 76
Mok, Ta, 101
murders, 9, 46, 62, 78–79, 95–96, 98

national assembly, 17, 22–23, 32, 52, 65–66
National Liberation Front, 42
National Party Congress, 84
Nixon, Richard M., 51–52
Nol, Lon, 39, 47, 49
    declares himself president of Cambodia, 52
    flees Phnom Penh, 60
    as prime minister, 55–56
    Sihanouk and, 53
North Vietnam, 42, 43, 53, 54, 58–59

Office 87, 99
Office 100, 41, 46, 47, 82

party congress, 36–37
People's Republic of Kampuchea, 92
Phnom Penh (Cambodia), 6, 14, 33, 56, 63
    evacuation of, by Khmer Rouge, 59–61, 61–62
Pol Pot (Saloth Sar)
    as acting secretary general, 37
    in Beijing, 44–46, 79
    builds new government, 64–66
    communism and, 18–21
    Communist Party and, 23, 24–25, 53, 56–58
    cult of personality and, 82–84
    death of, 101
    early life of, 9–10
    education of, 14–16, 17–18
    in exile, 90, 92, 94
    family of, 9–10, 36, 62
    Four-Year Plan and, 66–68
    genocide and, 77–78
    under house arrest, 101
    interview of, with foreign journalists, 86–89
    Khmer Rouge and, 99–100
    legacy of, 102
    as revolutionary, 34–36

marriage of, 33–34, 99
    in Paris, 18–20, 21–22
    in Phnom Penh, 24, 39, 63
    as prime minister, 66
    publishes article, 22–23
    purges by, 76–77
    remorse for murders and, 98–99
    as teacher, 32–33, 100
    Tou Samouth and, 26–27, 37
    on trial in absentia, 96–97
    trip to Yugoslavia, 20–21
    Vietnam and, 43, 58–59, 66, 72
Ponchaud, François, 94–95
Ponnary, Khieu, 22, 33–34, 99
protests, 16, 39
purges, 72, 76–77, 80–82, 84, 90

Ratanakiri, 47–48
refugees, 56, 85, 96
rice, 67

Samouth, Tou, 26–27, 37
Samphan, Khieu, 97
Samrin, Heng, 85, 92
Sangkum Party, 31, 39
Sann, Son, 97
Sar, Saloth. See Pol Pot
Saran, Ney, 76
Sary, Ieng, 17–18, 21, 34, 48, 55, 65
    on trial in absentia, 96–97
Sen, Son, 101
Sihanouk, Norodom, 5, 14, 17, 22–23, 29, 47
    allies with North Vietnam, 42
    Battambang uprising and, 49–50
    Cambodia and, 50–51, 90
    coalition government and, 97
    France and, 16–17, 26
    economic policies of, 38
    forms Sangkum Party, 31–32
    as head of state, 65

Pol Pot and, 40
    removed from office, 52
socialist system, 67
South Vietnam, 42, 46, 55, 58
Soviet Union, 19–20, 30, 66
Stalin, Joseph, 20, 66, 83

Thailand, 11, 12, 93, 94
Tito, Marshal, 20–21
Tuol Sleng prison, 6, 73–74, 75, 76–77, 96

United Front for the National Salvation of Kampuchea, 85
United States, 7, 94, 97–98
    Cambodia and, 51, 52, 55, 59
    evacuation of Phnom Penh and, 63
    Lon Nol and, 55–56
    Vietnam and, 42, 46, 58

Vannsak, Keng, 19, 21, 22, 23, 29, 31–32, 36
Vet, Vorn, 5–6
Vietminh, 25–26, 27, 29, 30, 41–42
Vietnam, 5, 7, 11, 12, 37
    Cambodia and, 30, 89, 92, 99
    division of, 28–29
    Khmer Rouge and, 79–80, 84
    Pol Pot and, 66, 72
    Soviet Union and, 30
    support of Samrin by, 85
Vietnamese Communists, 42, 44, 52, 55, 56–58
Vietnam War, 42–44, 46, 51–52, 58, 66

Workers' Party of Kampuchea, 37

Year Zero, 8, 61
Yugoslavia, 20–21

Zhou Enlai, 52, 90

Picture Credits

Cover Image: © Bettmann/CORBIS
AFP/Getty Images, 45
AP/Wide World Photos, 8, 81, 91, 95, 100
© Bettmann/CORBIS, 28, 32, 35, 41, 51, 55, 88
© Bohemian Nomad Picturemakers/CORBIS, 73, 75
© CENTRE DOC.DU CAMB/CORBIS SYGMA, 63
© Chris Rainier/CORBIS, 83
© Francoise de Mulder/CORBIS, 57
Jehangir Gazdar/Woodfin Camp/Time Life
  Pictures/Getty Images, 25
Keystone/Hulton Archive/Getty Images, 14
© Reuters/CORBIS, 18
© Richard Dudman/CORBIS SYGMA, 87
© The Bettmann Archive/CORBIS, 4